Emmy Budd
and the
Hijacked Train

Jean Blasiar

Emmy Budd and the Hijacked Train / Jean Blasiar
First Edition Paperback: April 2010
ISBN 978-1-936185-13-9
Editor: Reba Hilbert
Layout: Roger Hunt
Cover Design: Molly Courtright

Other books by Jean Blasiar:
Downtown Cowboy
Poor Rich

Coming soon from Jean Blasiar:
Emmy Budd - Don't Look Now
Emmy Budd - The Real Dog is Harry
Emmy Budd and the Gypsies
Emmy Budd and the Scarlet Scarf
Readers may contact the author at: www.JeanBlasiar.com

Published by Charles River Press, Inc.
541 Long Lane
Casper, Wyoming 82609

Printed in the United States of America

10   9   8   7   6   5   4   3   2   1

Acknowledgements

An Emmy-wink to the creative team at Charles River Press; Molly Courtright, Reba Hilbert, Roger Hunt and Jonathan Womack for their encouragement and commitment to this series.

Dedication

Emmy Budd is dedicated to girls and boys who lived in a simpler time when hometown adventure could be found waiting around every corner, especially to Edie, Rob, and Andy who grew up with me.

We met in a casual way, nothing remarkable to remind me later of the day or the hour. I do happen to recall that it was sundown, the time of day when the firemen lower the American flag on the courthouse lawn. I was watching this ceremony sitting on my bike, licking an ice-cream cone. Nothing unusual, nothing sensational, nothing extraordinary about the first time I ever laid eyes on the most exciting young person I ever met in my life, Thomas John Blake, T.J.

He was also sitting on his bike. Out of the corner of my eye I watched him watch me watch the fireman lower the flag, fold it neatly into a tight little triangle, walk ceremoniously back to the firehouse - tripping over the only rainbird on the courthouse lawn – and sprawl unceremoniously onto the wet grass.

The stranger on the purple bike never took his eyes off me. He watched me as I watched the fireman get up with the flag high over his head. The tight triangle never touched the wet ground.

"Did you know," I asked the handsome boy on the purple bike, "that in St. Louis in the early nineteen hundreds, there were only two automobiles in town, and they ran into each other."

The boy continued to stare at me, specifically at my long red pigtails—like honey to flies, baited hooks in a sea of innocent young boy fish. I flicked my pigtails over my shoulders seductively.

"You've got very nice hair," I thought he said.

"Thanks," I replied.

"For what?" he asked.

"For saying I have nice hair."

"I said, you've got ice cream in your hair."

"Oh."

"You probably got hair in your ice cream, too."

I looked at the cone.

"Throw it away," he suggested. "I'll buy you another one."

He turned and started to ride away. *The nerve of him*, I thought. I tossed the ice-cream cone in the metal container on the corner. He was looking back and waving for me to catch up.

Following T.J. was how I spent the rest of that summer, the most exciting, frightening, wonderful summer of my life.

T.J. loved and hated the same things I did. We loved three-way chili nine ways. We even talked Mrs. Blake, T.J.'s mom, who was a waitress at The Chili Bowl, into serving the "MT Special" (M for Em, T for Tommy), now a hot item on The Chili Bowl's menu: spaghetti, chili, beans, onions, cheese, avocado, sliced ripe olives, bacon bits, and sour cream.

Also, we discovered one dark and stormy afternoon while riding our bikes that we both loved thunderstorms. It was sticky and steamy, not unusual weather for Jerseyville in summer. After the first slam-banging bolt of lightning and earth-shaking thunder, I stopped riding my bike, threw my head back, and let the big welcome drops of rain run down my face and neck. T.J. told me it was then that he decided I was okay…for a girl.

The Blakes—T.J. and his mom—lived on the other side of town. The Courthouse Square was exactly halfway from their house to ours. That summer I was twelve and he was thirteen, I rode my bike to the flagpole in the square every morning about ten, met T.J., who always got there first, and took off, cruising the town for freebies.

Emmy Budd and the Hijacked Train

Swimming at the playground was free. I wore a T-shirt over my bathing suit to keep from being covered with "angel kisses," my dad's expression for freckles. I also wore the T-shirt because Debbie Farwell wore a bikini, and next to her, I looked more like T.J.

It didn't make me at all unhappy that Debbie Farwell was not the least bit interested in T.J. Not that she didn't think he was cute. She even said that she thought he was cute. Thick, curly brown hair, green eyes, freckles on his nose (like me), not too tall (like me), not too fat, and not too thin—not too anything but "too young," Debbie said. I told her what a fun guy he was, but that summer Debbie was only interested in guys who appreciated more sophisticated girls. T.J. said he liked to dunk a girl and see if anything important came off, like eyebrows or the color of her cheeks. He didn't actually come out and say so, but I was pretty sure that he didn't like Debbie Farwell. That didn't make me unhappy either.

The two of us swam a lot those first few weeks we were getting acquainted. I mean we SWAM. Laps! We didn't sunbathe or mess around. We worked out. I lost six pounds.

And we fished. Fishing was free. I never caught anything, but T.J. hooked a couple of little fish, which I made him throw back. He suggested that we take them down to The Chili Bowl, but I didn't have the nerve. Mrs. Blake would have skinned *us*.

4

JEAN Blasiar

T.J. got a book at the library (libraries are neat free places) on how to make paper gliders, and for almost a week we searched every morning for a higher place than the day before to sail our planes. The best place we found was the high school stadium. T.J. became so good at sailing paper airplanes that he could make them loop over the goalpost. I loved flying those planes with him.

The second craziest thing we did that summer was build a raft. T.J. got the idea for it when we found these poles (each one a different length, some of them split) that the hardware store put out for trash. T.J. talked Mr. Foster, the owner of the hardware store, into letting us have them. It didn't matter to Mr. Foster one way or the other who carted the poles away, us or the garbage truck, but after the fifth trip on our bikes from the hardware store to the creek at the edge of town, I began to wonder if it was such a terrific idea after all. T.J. was so excited about it; I had to go along.

The rope to tie the poles together was one of our few investments that summer. I had four dollars; T.J. had three. It took almost all of it to buy the sturdiest nylon rope we could find. Mr. Foster even gave us a discount, probably because we told him that we were building a fence for a neighbor who was crippled. I doubt we would have gotten the discount if we had told him we were building a raft. Maybe he wouldn't even have let us take the poles. My guess is he wouldn't.

Emmy Budd and the Hijacked Train

T.J. tied the poles together in a half hitch or a hitch or a slide or something he learned as a Scout; anyway, they held. It took half a day to get all the poles to the creek bed and almost the other half to lay them out, figure which one went where (all of them different lengths), tie and tie knots until I thought my fingers had permanent grooves in two joints. It was just about sundown when *The Unsinkable MT* (our forever and for everything coat of arms) was ready to launch.

T.J. saved one long pole to push off the side. The pond wasn't that wide or that deep. We were never really in any danger even if we fell in or capsized, but we pretended that we were. We were the *African Queen*, the first white settlers in hostile Indian territory, Tarzan and Jane, Robinson Crusoe and Friday, and a name that I was afraid might stick, Tom Sawyer and "Huck," and you know who was Huck.

What we were hoping for that first launch when it was almost dark was a raging thunderstorm. We could ride the frightening sea, pit ourselves against the fierce waves, cling to the poles for our very lives, but all we had was a gentle wind that cooled the air and made it only delightful, not life threatening.

"My jeans are soaked," I announced after our first round-trip. I also remarked, "It isn't very comfortable, is it?"

JEAN Blasiar

T.J. looked at me, exasperated. "Female!" he shouted. I came to know it as his curse word.

My bottom hurt. My fingers ached. I wasn't comfortable sitting or lying or kneeling, especially kneeling, but I smiled. It was wonderful.

"We can hide it in the bushes," T.J. said. "Cover it with leaves and come back every day for a float down the river."

"River" was an exaggeration. "Lake" was an exaggeration. "Old swimming hole" is what it had been before it got too murky even for that. For the first time since we met, I began to wonder if this was how I wanted to spend the summer, with a boy on a raft.

"We could bring some pillows," I suggested.

"And you could make curtains," T.J. said disgustedly. "You're a FEMALE, just like my mother."

"I am *not* a *FEMALE*!" I mean, how ridiculous.

T.J. was staring at me.

"I mean, I am a female, but not like your mother."

"What's wrong with my mother?"

"Nothing."

"Well…there is."

"What?"

"She's never happy any place we live. We move every two years, not just houses, but towns, different parts of the country. Did I tell you that we used to live in Florida?"

"No," I said. "You didn't." I didn't know very much at all about Tommy John Blake and his mother actually, even though we'd spent every day for over a month together. "Did you like Florida?"

"No. But I did swim every day."

I hesitated, but I had to know. "Do you like it here?"

He looked at me and I went all...*female.* "Yes," he said, sending funny little sensations through my body.

"I guess I better go," I said, not wanting to.

"Yeah," he said. "I guess." He helped me off the raft and I helped him hide it in the bushes.

The next day we rode the raft again. And the day after that. And the day after that. By that third day I walked like I'd been riding a horse most of my life. It hurt to walk straight or even bend my knees.

I was glad that my dad was away on a trip to the West Coast. We did things together, my dad and I—basketball in the evenings in our side yard, bowling or softball on the weekends with some kids from school. Dad likes to get out and exercise on weekends. He sure would have noticed how funny I walked. Nothing much escapes him. Mom didn't seem to notice anything but how much I was growing and how many new clothes I would need for school. School and new clothes were two things I wouldn't even talk about. Period.

The fourth morning after we built the raft, I was sur-

JEAN Blasiar

prised that T.J. wasn't waiting for me at the flagpole at ten o'clock. He hadn't missed a morning until then. I wondered devilishly if maybe he was having trouble getting out of bed also, but as I sat on my bike wondering how long I should wait and whether I should phone him if he didn't show up, I spotted his bike racing toward me. He came to a screeching halt, leaving a skid mark about twenty feet long. His legs couldn't be hurting, like mine.

"Em!" he blurted out excitedly. "I have a great idea!"

Superman didn't know how unadventurous Lois Lane was feeling. Still, I was willing to consider anything but climbing back on the raft.

"I don't want to spoil it until I show you," T.J. said, turning his bike around. "Follow me." He was a good fifty feet away before I managed to get my unbending knees moving again. I felt like the Tin Man before Dorothy found the oil can.

"What's the matter with you?" T.J. called, turning around and coming back for me. "Are you stiff?"

"Are you kidding?" I yelled back. "I'm sunburned." I was that, also.

He smiled that little grin of his. "Why, I never would have known."

"Go on. Go on. I'm coming."

"And I thought you were just blushing."

"Will you move it!"

Oooh, that boy. After three days of doing not much of anything but sitting on the raft and sailing the wild sea, T.J. knew everything there was to know about me and I knew just about everything there was to know about him. We both told the darnedest things about ourselves, nothing I regretted, but a lot I never told anyone else. Frankly, I about ran out of things to tell T.J. Blake, and I think he was running out of things to tell me. The last thing I wanted to happen was that we would start to bore each other. Seeing him racing ahead excitedly on a new kick kept my aching legs pedaling.

T.J. stopped at the train yard. I couldn't see anything very exciting happening. The Commodore was in the station, about a block away from where T.J. pulled up. He was staring at the back of the train.

"Fascinating," I said sarcastically.

"Keep watching," T.J. urged, never taking his eyes off the last car. Two men in a jeep drove up and started putting mailbags and boxes into the last car on the tracks.

"The baggage car?" I said. "Is that what you're watching?"

"Shush," T.J. growled. He turned to look at me. "Are you watching?" he asked sharply. Obviously, I was missing something.

"What?" I whispered. "Give me a hint."

His eyes glared at me as he pointed to the baggage car. I watched the two men load the car, watched them climb back into the jeep and ride along the train until they came to the dock where passengers were boarding. The station was about a block away from where we sat on our bikes.

"At the risk of sounding really stupid," I said, "what am I supposed to see?"

T.J. stared at me. I was not sharing his enthusiasm for this wonderful event. "Emmy," he said slowly, "what's happening up there at the station?"

I grinned. He was playing games with me. "People are getting on the train?" I said.

"And who's in the baggage car?" T.J. said, father to child, big brother to little sister, genius to stoop.

"Who?" I said. "No one." At ten o'clock the sun was already blistering my already blistered face. "Can we leave?" I asked impatiently.

"Em!" T.J. shouted. "Where are you today? Don't you see the opportunity here? There is no one, *NO ONE*, in that baggage car. And everyone—look at them, Em, up at the station—*EVERYONE* is up there with the passengers. Nobody is paying any attention to the baggage car once it's loaded. Now…do you know where that train is going, Em?"

"Where?"

"Pittsburgh."

"That's in Pennsylvania."

"Very good, Emmy Budd."

"Thanks."

"Don't mention it."

"I won't."

"EMMY!"

"What? I'm sunburned! Can't we stand in the shade at least and talk about this?"

T.J. jerked me and my bike over into the shadow of the station's large oak trees.

"Better?" he said angrily. I nodded. "Have you ever been to Pittsburgh?" he asked coolly.

I shook my head. Suddenly, I had this crazy idea that T.J. was suggesting we hop on the baggage car and ride The Commodore to Pittsburgh.

"Why don't we go," he whispered.

"You're crazy. You're absolutely crazy. And the craziest thing about it is, I think you're serious."

"I am. Listen. I don't mean right now. Tomorrow. We can hide our bikes in these bushes and sneak on board *after* they load the baggage car. See how much time there is?"

That's what he was doing. He was suggesting that we run away to Pittsburgh.

"I checked the schedule this morning. The Commodore lays over two hours in Pittsburgh. We can catch the two-thirty baggage car back to Jerseyville."

JEAN Blasiar

He wasn't asking me to run away to Pittsburgh forever…only for the day.

I'd never been on a train before. Suddenly, the adventure of it, the excitement of taking a train anywhere got to me, too. What was it we were doing? Hoboing! That's it! Hoboing! Not terribly illegal…I guess.

"Why not!" I said agreeably.

T.J. punched me in the shoulder affectionately, the sunburned shoulder. "Tomorrow, Em," he said excitedly. "Tomorrow we'll go to Pittsburgh."

He turned his bike around. "You're terrific, Em," he said, shaking his head and making a little admiring sound with his teeth. "Let's go to the pond."

Three

The all-time craziest thing I have ever done in my life, so far, was sneaking on board The Commodore with T.J. Blake. Certainly it was the craziest thing we did that summer.

Everything else about the morning was normal. Mother was out in the garden pruning roses as usual when I left the house on my bike.

"Good-bye, Emmy Lu," she called. "Watch out for busy streets." She should have known what busy streets I'd be crossing. In Pittsburgh!

T.J. was waiting for me at the courthouse. He looked calm, but when he spoke I could tell that he was as nervous as I was.

"Did you bring anything to eat?" he asked. I heard his voice shake. I knew then, for sure, that he was nervous, like me. I showed him a beef jerky in my jeans pocket and a candy bar.

"Good," he said. "Don't forget to put the wrapper from the candy bar back in your pocket. We don't want to leave any clues that we've been there." He was beaming. "We might want to do it again sometime," he said, grinning.

JEAN Blasiar

I giggled. He was such a cute guy. I loved the way his hair swept across his forehead. A couple of wisps curled around his ears that morning, just long enough to be cute. He was wearing jeans also and a plaid shirt. We both wore running shoes. I thought, as I glanced nervously at our feet, that we might both need good running shoes before this day was over.

We hid our bikes in the bushes alongside the stationhouse, just as T.J. planned.

"Did you lock it?" he whispered, and I nodded. He motioned for me to follow him.

"Try not to be conspicuous," he said.

"Are you kidding?" I whispered. With two flaming red pigtails, I can't be inconspicuous no matter what I do.

T.J. pulled something out of his pocket and handed it to me. "Put this on," he said. It was a gray engineer's cap.

"You think of everything." I piled my pigtails on top of my head and put on the cap. It was snug, but it fit. "Where'd you get it?" I asked.

"Marshall's," he whispered back. He was watching the stationhouse intently. He glanced back at me, at my hair. "That's better," he said, taking my hand.

We waited about fifteen minutes quietly, except for an occasional giggle from me, until two men in a jeep drove up. One man got out and carried three large mailbags into

15

the baggage car; then he got back in the jeep and the two of them drove back to the station's loading dock.

T.J. kept his eye on the jeep as it headed toward the platform. Suddenly he tugged on my hand hard.

"Let's go," he said firmly, and I crept alongside him until we came to a path in the bushes. We were directly opposite the baggage car.

The minute I set foot on the steps of that baggage car I became frightened, more frightened than I've ever been in my life. T.J. helped me up and we stepped inside.

The baggage car was deserted. It was full of railroad spikes and pieces of wood. The three large mailbags were piled in one corner.

We sat down on the floor behind a couple of empty barrels. I was sitting on a large bag of spikes or nails or something.

"What if they come back with more mail?" I asked.

T.J. jabbed me in the ribs with his elbow, but lightly. "Sh-h-h," he said, putting a finger to his lips.

Metal gates were closing. Someone called, "All aboard!" and we began to move. I leaned over and whispered, "It isn't very comfortable, is it?"

T.J. turned and glared at me. "Maybe you'd like to ring for a pillow."

"That would be very nice," I said. Suddenly, I thought of something. "T.J.," I practically screamed.

JEAN Blasiar

"Keep your voice down!"

"But what if they don't have a mail car coming back to Jerseyville?"

My cute hoboing friend leaned over, jabbed me in the ribs, and told me to "eat your beef, jerk."

Four

It took awhile to get settled with the bouncing around. I was almost enjoying the click, clack, click, clack, click, clack, not that I could stand up and walk without being knocked around from side to side.

There was a window in the back of the baggage car, but neither T.J. nor I had the courage to get up and look out.

"Pittsburgh's big, right," I asked.

T.J. nodded. "You bet," he said.

"You ever been there?"

"No, but I see it a lot on TV. The Pirates."

"Oh, sure, the Pirates. What else?"

"Well…the Steelers. Got to be a big city with the Steelers and the Pirates."

I laughed.

"What's funny?"

"The Steelers, the Pirates," I said, "and the hobos."

T.J. grinned. "It's going to be fun," he said confidently.

We sat listening to the clicking and the clacking for a few more minutes. "Where do you think we are?" I asked.

T.J. shrugged.

JEAN Blasiar

"We're probably still in Jerseyville, right?"

"I don't know," T.J. said. "Want me to look out the window?"

"No. What if we're passing through a town and somebody sees you?"

"Yeah."

I sat there, bouncing on the hard floor, but I thought that I shouldn't remark again how uncomfortable it was. It reminded me a lot of the raft.

T.J. appeared to be listening for something. "Does it seem to you like we're stopping?" he said.

I put my hands, palms down, on the floor. "You're the Scout," I said. "Put your ear to the floor or something."

"Sh-h-h."

T.J. was right. The train was definitely slowing down.

"You think it's a crossing?"

T.J. shook his head. "We're stopping," he said. "We weren't supposed to stop until we get to Pittsburgh."

"Is it Pittsburgh already?"

T.J. shook his head again. I grabbed his arm.

"Do you suppose they know we're on the train?" I looked up at the ceiling and the walls of the car. "Maybe it's bugged," I whispered. "Maybe they've heard us talking back here."

T.J. didn't say anything, but I could tell by the way his

eyes darted around the car that he wondered, too. "Don't be scared," he said reassuringly, but he knew I was scared and I knew he was scared.

The train came to a complete stop. I glanced at the window.

"Wait here," T.J. said. "I'm going to take a peek."

Reluctantly I let go of his hand, but I crawled along after him. "Not without me," I said.

T.J. stood up first and looked out.

"What do you see?" I whispered from my crouch on the floor.

"Nothing," T.J. said. "We're in the middle of a cornfield."

"Have we broken down?"

What a horrible thought that was. Maybe they'd have to evacuate the train, move the baggage to another car. "Oh!" I cried.

"Sh-h-h, quiet!"

T.J. was trying to listen to something outside. He moved to the other side of the window. "There's a car out there," he muttered, "a black car."

"A railroad car?" I asked.

"An automobile," he said. He pulled me up so I could see. "Don't let anyone see you," he said.

We were right smack in the middle of a cornfield. Corn

20

to the right of us, corn to the left of us, corn behind us, and, I assumed, corn ahead of us.

"What are we doing here?" I asked nervously.

"There's somebody in that black car," T.J. said, pointing to the left side of the window.

T.J. moved aside so I could see. The bill of my cap was pressed against the window, a very small window, but I did manage to spot the car.

"Is it the police?" I asked. "Maybe they radioed ahead that we were here and the police have come to take us off the train."

T.J. was staring out the window. He never took his eyes off what he was watching.

"It's two men," he said suddenly. "EM!" he cried. "They've got guns! *SHOTGUNS!*"

"Oh, no!" I cried. "Put your hands up, T.J." I put mine up.

"They're not police," T.J. said. His eyes were as big as marbles.

"T.J., I'm scared!"

He put his arm around me. I still had my hands up in the air. "Put your hands up," I urged him again, "in case they come in after us."

"One of them has an axe," T.J. said.

"An axe?" I screamed.

"Sh-h-h." T.J. pulled me down to the floor. "Keep quiet now," he said, putting a hand over my mouth. "They're walking this way."

We were huddled close together, so close that I could feel T.J.'s breath on my neck. I couldn't tell if it was *his* heart beating or mine.

We could hear the men walking on a gravel path along-side our car. I closed my eyes. They wouldn't shoot kids, would they?

It was absolutely still. The only sound was the footsteps on the gravel outside. Someone once told me that if you stand in a field of corn and keep absolutely quiet, you could hear the corn growing. Isn't that a dumb thing to be thinking about, with two men creeping up on you carry-ing shotguns and an axe?

I heard them walk on and on and on until we couldn't hear them anymore. I opened my eyes and looked at T.J. He wasn't looking at me, but I could tell he was listening.

"Listen," he said after a long while. "Hear that?"

I strained to hear. "What?" I said. I did hear something, but couldn't make out what it was.

T.J. looked squarely at me. "They're axing the rails up ahead," he said suddenly. "Em! We're being hijacked!"

"WHAT?"

"Hijacked!"

I stared at him. I put my fingers to his face. *He* was real. *This* was real.

JEAN Blasiar

"They're robbers," Tommy said. "I have to see." He jumped up and I slipped to the floor.

"Don't go out there!" I screamed, but he walked to the door and peeked out.

"T.J.!"

He motioned for me to be quiet. He picked up a handful of spikes and a large block of wood. He shoved the spikes into his pocket. "Come with me," he said.

I felt like I had legs of iron, but I needed to hold his hand. I jumped up and stumbled until I got to his side.

"I'm so scared," I admitted.

"I know, I know," T.J. said. "Sh-h-h." He led me outside. First, he stepped down one step and looked up the right side of the train.

"What do you see?" I whispered.

He stepped back up. "Nothing," he said. He walked around me and stepped down on the first step on the other side of the car.

"Well?" I was so nervous, but T.J. shook his head.

"Nothing," he said again. He looked back toward the black automobile parked behind the train in the corn-field. "They must be inside the coaches."

"Do you think they'll come back here?" I whispered.

"Em," T.J. said seriously. He was so serious. I was shaking like a pup in a cold rain. "Em," he said again, "there's something we have to do. Take my hand."

I followed him. I don't know how or why, but I let him

23

lead me off that train on the same side as the black auto-mobile. Quickly we ran across the gravel and into the tall corn.

I did feel a lot better once I was off the train and hiding in the corn. It was taller than we were. Thank you, God, I remember saying, for a good year for corn. And thank you for this gray cap that's hiding my red hair in this cornfield.

T.J. was heading straight for the black car. It was an old car. "T.J., what are you doing?" I shouted.

He didn't say anything. He just kept making his way until we were standing right beside that car. Then he bent down and with the piece of wood he pounded spikes into the back tire.

"Are you crazy?" I whispered hoarsely. "Let's get out of here!"

T.J. crept behind the car to the other rear tire and pounded spikes into it. I was certain that any minute I would feel a gun in my back, that somehow they would sneak up behind us without my seeing them and shoot us both.

T.J. grabbed my hand and began running with me back to the train. I was shaking so badly that I couldn't find a voice to scream. I tried to pull him into the tall corn to hide, but he was running faster and faster back to the baggage car.

We darted quickly over the gravel and up the steps

again. T.J. grabbed me when we were safely behind the barrels and dragged me down to the floor. He picked up a tarpaulin and threw it over both of us.

"Don't say a word," he said, panting.

I was breathing so hard and so fast that T.J. put a hand over my mouth and nose. Finally, I had to jerk it away. I couldn't breathe. It was a hundred and ten under that tarp.

We were there fifteen minutes at least. Neither of us said a word. Suddenly, we heard footsteps running along the gravel again. They were close. I knew they were going to rob the baggage car next.

Under the tarp, they couldn't see that we were just kids. If we moved, if we made them suspicious, they'd probably shoot first and then look and see who or what we were. With that awful thought in mind, I never even took a breath. I heard one of the men yell, "Turn that car around!"

We were suffocating. T.J. pulled back the tarp and we both took a welcome breath. Perspiration was running down T.J.'s face. My eyes burned, my throat hurt, my chest hurt, everything throbbed until I thought my heart would explode.

T.J. crept along the floor to the back window. He waved his hand for me to follow him, but I couldn't move. I watched him inch his way slowly up the wall to the window.

"There's three of them, Em," he whispered.

All I could wonder was where that other man had come from. What if he'd seen T.J. pounding nails into their tires? I couldn't stand it there alone. Like slow motion I moved a knee at a time until I made my way to T.J. When I looked up at him, I was terrified by the scared look on his face.

"They can't turn the car around, Em," T.J. murmured. "It's wobbling all over the place. They can't even push it." He continued to watch them. He pulled me up. "Take a look," he said.

I wasn't sure my knees would hold me up. I sneaked up on the window carefully. Imagine what those guys would do if they spotted us watching them, realizing that we had caused trouble with their car. I lifted my head to the window only as far as my eyes.

The only thing I saw was the car wobbling wildly. A man was standing on the outside, pushing. He began kicking the front wheel.

"Listen, Em, listen!" T.J. said excitedly, but all I could really hear was my own heartbeat. There was some sort of faint hum in the background. It got louder and louder and *louder* and suddenly so loud that I wanted to grab my ears and scream.

"WHAT IS IT?" I shouted.

"A helicopter," T.J. said excitedly. "It's the police."

JEAN Blasiar

It was a helicopter. I recognized the sound. And it was right on top of us.

While T.J. continued to watch, I slipped back down to the floor. My legs were wobbly. I couldn't have run if my life depended on it.

T.J. shouted, "Hear the sirens, Em? Hear them?" He was so excited. I couldn't have pried him away from that window.

"The helicopter is right over the black car, Em."

The noise was awful. Suddenly, T.J. ducked down to the floor. "Those crazy fools, Em. They're shooting at the helicopter. Don't they hear those sirens coming?"

I heard something that sounded like gunfire, but with all the other noises, the helicopter and the shrill siren in the background, it was impossible to be sure.

T.J. was saying something. I could see his lips moving. He'd creep up and take a look and then pop down to the floor and yell something at me that I never quite got.

What I wanted to do was *SCREAM*! No one would have heard me. There were people running along the gravel path and sirens everywhere. T.J. was watching very carefully out the window. With all the intense noise and excitement outside, it was awhile before we realized that the train had begun to move.

I clutched T.J.'s legs. He had one hand on my head. Finally, I could hear him again.

"We're backing up, Em," he said. "Back to Jerseyville."

It was the best news all morning. We were heading home. It felt like we'd been gone a week. My clothes were stuck to my body. T.J. slipped down to the floor beside me.

We just sat there huddled together below the window, swaying gently to the noise of the train. I wanted to go to sleep but I thought that if I close my eyes, the next thing I know I could be awakened by someone who discovers us. We couldn't be discovered now. I wasn't sure what we were—fugitives, stowaways—whatever laws we'd broken. For sure, nobody was going to be waiting in Jerseyville to pin any medals on us.

I will never forget the sensation of that ride back to Jerseyville in my life. Even today, when I back up in a car, I start to get hot, my stomach gets queasy, and I'm positive I'm going to be sick.

He didn't say so, but I knew that T.J. never dreamed we might *"back"* into the Jerseyville station. Just where the baggage car would stop in the train yard was a big mystery.

T.J. leaned over and whispered in my ear, "So how did you like Pittsburgh?"

The dope.

Five

The train stopped, but we didn't move, either of us. After a while, T.J. let go of my hand and inched up the wall to the window.

"Where are we?" I asked softly.

T.J. shook his head. "I don't know, but we have to get off before they search the train."

"What if we're not in Jerseyville?"

"We have to get off anyway."

I followed T.J. across the floor of the car on my hands and knees. My knees certainly took a beating that summer.

The air outside the baggage car was cool and fresh against my wet skin. Perspiration dripped down the sides of the cap that held my hair.

T.J. put one foot on the steps and looked out. "When I say 'go,'" he said, grabbing my hand. He said it before I was ready. "Go!"

My legs moved but my feet were like lead. I tried not to make any noise as we walked quickly across the ground.

We were on the other side of the station from where we

boarded. About fifty feet ahead we were able to duck into some bushes.

It smelled like Jerseyville. It felt like Jerseyville, but nothing looked familiar. T.J. kept pulling me along.

I took off my cap. T.J. stuck it inside his shirt. Perspiration ran down my forehead.

There were men in blue uniforms running around everywhere. I saw the train engineer waving his hands wildly and pointing toward Pittsburgh. Pittsburgh.

The Steelers, the Pirates, and the robbers. I mean…who would believe it?

When we reached the station, we sort of mingled with the crowd. I saw a woman fanning herself with a magazine, telling a policeman what had happened.

"They took my jewelry," she said, fanning herself wildly. "Right off my fingers. Just pulled my rings right off my fingers." She showed the policeman her bare hand. "And my watch. I had to give them my watch. And my wallet, my checkbook. They got it all. Oh…what am I going to tell my husband about my checkbook?"

"Don't worry, lady," the policeman said, trying to calm her. "You'll get all of your things back just as soon as we book these guys. You can claim them later at police headquarters. Everything will be returned to you."

He put his hands up and shouted to the crowd. "Did you

hear that, everybody? Everything will be returned to you. No reason for anybody to panic. We got the men and all the things they took from you people. If you'll all just come into the waiting room so the officers can get your names and addresses. Move inside please, folks. Try to tell the officers just what it was that you lost. Be as specific as you can. What kind of watch was it? Any inscription? Anything that can help identify your property. Okay, folks?"

The crowd became noisy in the confusion, everyone talking at once, but they moved slowly into the waiting room. T.J. and I watched them. We hung around long enough to walk around them and get to our bikes.

I was sure, absolutely sure, that while we were walking so slowly, so casually away from the station, someone was going to stop us. A whistle blew and my heart nearly leapt through my chest. I froze.

"Keep walking," T.J. said calmly. "Pretend you didn't hear it."

Somehow I managed to go on. I was so glad to see my bike that I fell on the ground beside it. T.J. knew the combination and unlocked it for me.

"Come on," he urged. "Don't stop till we get to the pond."

He started to walk his bike. Just putting my hands on the handlebars gave me a good feeling. It was my bike, my town. I thought that I would never as long as I lived want to leave it again. I walked my bike down the path behind T.J.

"Easy," T.J. said softly. "No quick moves, just very casual. Don't go through any stop signs or red lights."

He didn't have to tell me.

On the ride to the pond, I was certain that any minute someone would blow a whistle again and big hands would swoop down on me and stop me from going any farther. T.J. looked back several times to see if I was still coming. He reached the pond first. I watched him jump off his bike, letting it fall, run to the water, and scoop water into his face. Then, dreamlike, I got off my bike, carefully put the kickstand in place, walked over to the pond, knelt down, and felt the water.

T.J. looked over at me and laughed. He sprinkled water in my face. The cool water was real. Everything else was kind of gray.

"Em…you all right?" T.J. must have asked me several times before I heard him. Finally, he shook me. "Em?"

"I'm…okay," I said. The sound of my own voice. When was the last time I heard it?

"You sure?"

I nodded.

"You're not getting sick?"

"No."

JEAN Blasiar

"Splash some more water on your face." He was staring at me. "Eat your candy bar, Em."

That was a good idea. I reached into my jeans pocket. The candy bar was smashed, but I ripped off the wrapper and took a bite. I offered some to T.J.

"Thanks. I have one." He reached into his own pocket and pulled out a small bar.

The candy was good. The chewing helped. My jaw felt stiff. Everything felt stiff.

"Do you believe it?" T.J. said. "Did you hear them at the station? I was standing right next to this guy who was telling two policemen about the robbery. He talked about the guns. They held guns on them when they robbed them, Em. It was armed robbery."

Calling it that…armed robbery…made me sick again.

"Imagine, Em," T.J. was saying, "imagine what would have happened if they'd caught us spiking their tires."

I shivered.

"They might have shot us," T.J. said.

I was sure I was going to be sick.

"We can never tell anyone," T.J. said. He took off his shoes and socks and put his feet into the pond.

I don't know why I was thinking about it, but I said, "Why did the train stop in the first place?"

T.J. stretched out on the ground, his feet in the water, his hands behind his head.

"That third guy," T.J. said. "He must have been on the train."

I looked at him, shocked. "You mean he got on in Jerseyville?"

"Sure. Had to. How else could they stop a train? He had to threaten the engineer, or someone. He waited until we were near that cornfield. The car was waiting for him there."

"What if one of them had been hiding in the baggage car when we got on the train? What if we'd walked into that car and found a man with a gun hiding in there?"

T.J. put his hands over his eyes. "We might have been hostages," he said.

I put my head between my knees.

"You're not getting sick?"

I shook my head. I was pretty sure I would be.

"Want to ride the raft?"

No, I didn't. "Okay," I heard myself say.

I watched him, excited as always getting the raft ready for our adventure on the wild river.

"It didn't *really* happen," I said to myself. "It didn't really happen. It didn't really happen."

Six

Neither one of us felt like riding the raft. I felt sick. T.J. only felt hungry.

"Let's go to The Chili Bowl and ask Mom to feed us," he suggested eagerly. He was already sitting on his bike. Slowly, carefully, I followed him.

There was quite a lunch crowd in The Chili Bowl.

"Have you heard the news?" Mrs. Blake said excitedly as we sat down at the counter. "The Commodore was held up!" It did really happen. My stomach flipped.

"Mike Evans of the *Chronicle* was just in here," Mrs. Blake said. "He told me everything. They got two guys in the courthouse jail right now."

T.J. and I both shouted, *"TWO?"* at the same time.

Mrs. Blake looked at us so curiously that I thought for sure we had given ourselves away. "Two," she repeated. "One man got away. They're looking for him now."

"Where?" T.J. asked hoarsely.

"Here. In town," Mrs. Blake said. "Evidently he had a knife hidden up his sleeve or somewhere, and he pulled it on Officer Craig."

"Did he...did he kill him?" T.J. asked nervously.

"No," his mom said, "but he's in the hospital with a knife wound in the stomach."

I grabbed my mouth.

"Not here!" T.J. cried, rushing me to the door. "Bye, Mom," he called back. "Em isn't feeling so hot."

We ran down the street, leaving our bikes in front of the restaurant. I fell down on the courthouse lawn, burying my head in the cool, tall grass. "I'm not going to get sick," I said over and over again. "I'm not going to get sick!"

"Are you going to get sick?" T.J. asked.

"YES!"

I thought he would leave. He didn't.

"No," I said more calmly. It was better, lying down I mean, better than sitting at that counter smelling chili. I rolled over on my back.

"I could get you a soft drink," T.J. suggested politely. He's so cute.

"Thanks," I said. "Don't bother. I'm going to be okay."

T.J. sat down on the grass next to me. The look on his face frightened me. He was worried. I knew he was worried. I'd never seen him worried before, except on the train.

"You're worried," I said.

"Me? No."

"Yes, you are. You're worried."

"I'm not." He picked up a piece of grass and started pulling at it. "I'm scared," he admitted.

36

And that *really* scared me. That he was scared. "Would you recognize any of those men if you saw them again?" I asked.

T.J. shook his head, tossed the piece of grass in the air. "I don't know," he said. "I got a good look at one of them, the guy who was kicking the wheel. I think he looked right at me once."

"AT YOU?"

"At the back window. I don't know if he saw me or not, but he stared at the window."

"Oh, T.J., what if he did?"

"Don't, Em," T.J. said. "Don't panic." His voice was calm. His face still looked worried, but his voice was calm. I knew he was trying to calm me down also. "They'll find him," T.J. said with not a whole lot of confidence. "Maybe the guy who saw me in the window is one of the guys in jail right now."

"And maybe he isn't," I argued.

"Well, they'll find him. The whole police force is probably out looking for him."

T.J. stood up. "Let's walk back and get our bikes," he said. "You okay now?"

I nodded, stood up, and brushed the grass off my pants. "This is going to make a great story to tell our grandchildren someday."

Oh, no, I thought. *What did I just say?* "I mean," I

added quickly, "you telling your grandchildren and me telling my grandchildren."

T.J. was staring at me with a stupid look on his face. "I'll walk you home," he said.

We didn't talk much on the way home. We didn't talk at all about the robbery. I can't even remember what we did talk about. I would have been very happy to discuss the weather or anything else, forget the whole thing for a while, go up to my room and listen to some music, but our bad luck continued. Debbie Farwell was just riding out of my driveway on her bike as T.J. and I turned the corner of the street, and she spotted us. I heard T.J. groan behind me.

"Emmy!" Debbie called. "There you are!"

There was no escaping her once we turned the corner.

"What have you two been up to?" Debbie asked suspiciously, eyeing both of us.

"Just riding around," I lied.

Debbie stared at me and then at T.J. "Oh?" she said in that obnoxious way she has sometimes. She waited for us to say something more, but we didn't.

"Just riding around *where?*" she asked finally.

I turned to T.J. "Why don't you come in and have a drink," I suggested, ignoring Debbie's question. "You haven't met my mother yet, have you?"

I could tell that T.J. really didn't want to meet anyone

38

just then, but, good Scout that he is, he said, "Okay," and that he'd come in for a minute. Debbie, of course, followed.

We parked our bikes in the driveway and walked down to the side door. Mom was in the kitchen when we came in.

"Mom," I said, "this is Tommy Blake. T.J. He's…" I hesitated. "He's new in town."

Funny. There were so many things I could have said about Tommy Blake. He's my best friend. He's the person I spend all my time with, did you know? He's the boy who went with me to Pittsburgh this morning. But I said, "He's new in town." Which told her nothing.

T.J. said "Hello" to my mother and she said "Hello" to him. I got some drinks out of the refrigerator and took them out to the patio. The three of us were sitting at the table outside with our drinks when my mother came out and joined us.

"Did you hear about The Commodore?" she asked unexpectedly.

My hand slipped on the wet bottle of soda and I spilled most of it in my lap and on the table.

"Good one, Em," Debbie remarked, jumping up and running inside for some napkins.

"We just heard about it," T.J. said casually to my mother. He's such a cool guy, always covering for me. A really neat guy.

"What happened to The Commodore?" Debbie had to ask.

And so my mother told her the whole story. It was surprising how many details she knew. A couple of times I almost added to it, but fortunately caught myself in time. T.J. was staring at me uncomfortably.

"My gosh!" Debbie said when Mother finished. "Gosh" is not Debbie's usual expletive. "You mean there's a train robber loose in Jerseyville?" Debbie gushed. "My gosh!"

Mom was looking at me curiously. "I was beginning to worry about where you were, Emmy," she said.

I shrugged. "No place special," I said, looking at T.J. apologetically. It was *very* special, but it was also time to change the subject.

"What time is it?" I asked.

Debbie was waiting for someone to ask. It was probably the only reason she came over in the first place—a new watch, with diamonds and everything.

I grinned. "Nice," I said. She was holding it up under my nose. "What time is it?"

"Can't you tell time?"

"It doesn't have any numbers."

"Expensive ones don't."

"Thank you for explaining that."

"There's a diamond for the twelve, three, six, and nine."

I looked down at the watch again. "Well…it's either

JEAN Blasiar

half past two diamonds, or two diamonds past six. The hands are the same size, but I guess that's the way they are on expensive watches."

"You dingy!" Debbie cried. "It's four-thirty."

T.J. stood up quickly, as if he'd been waiting for the opportunity. "That late!" he exclaimed. "I have to go."

But Debbie hadn't finished with T.J. yet. "There must have been lots of police cars downtown," she said, tilting her head and staring at him. "Funny you didn't hear anything about the robbery."

It was my mother who saved T.J. from any further explanation. "How far do you live, Tommy?" she asked.

T.J. told her exactly where he lived, and, before she could ask, he also told her that he went to Franklin Junior High.

Debbie laughed. "Franklin?" she screamed. "I hope you aren't on the volleyball team." She grinned at me. "We beat them so bad every year."

It was too late to try to explain anything to T.J. now. I hadn't planned on telling him that I was on just about every boy's team there was at school, including the volleyball team. I think it would have made a difference how he felt about me. I *know* it would have made a difference how he felt about me. He certainly wouldn't have thought of me as *FEMALE*.

"I don't know anything about it," T.J. admitted. "I only started Franklin last January."

I knew T.J. didn't like Debbie. His dislike showed very much that afternoon, I thought. Debbie was probably too curious about the two of us to notice anything else, but I noticed. T.J. barely looked at Debbie.

"We *know* you don't have a very good volleyball team, don't we, Emmy?"

I didn't say anything. *How could anyone be so rude*, I thought. There were times, like then, that I wondered how Debbie Farwell and I could have remained friends for so long. When we were alone, she was so different. But when a boy was around, look out!

"Look at that!" Debbie cried suddenly. "If I didn't just get a snag in my nail. Do you have a file I could borrow, Mrs. Budd?"

After my mother left the patio to get the file, Debbie examined her nail more closely.

"Damnit!" she murmured. *That* was more like the real Debbie. I saw T.J. looking at her.

"I gotta go," he said again.

"I'll walk you out," I offered.

Debbie stood up also. "Wait for me, you two." She thanked my mother for the file, which she used while T.J. and I walked to the bikes. T.J. was shaking his head.

"She's okay." I defended her. "Just spoiled."

"And nosy," T.J. added.

JEAN Blasiar

I grinned. "Wouldn't she love to know about today," I said.

"Keep cool," T.J. warned me. "And quiet."

"And you be careful," I said. "If you see anybody who looks like that guy, you tell somebody."

"I will," he promised. Then he grinned. "I'll tell you."

"Hey! Wait up!"

Before Debbie caught up with us, I whispered to T.J. "This is really your lucky day. She's going your way."

Seven

They didn't catch the third man like T.J. was so certain they would. Mom was listening to the radio as I came down to breakfast the next morning.

"Now there's a killer on the loose in Jerseyville," she said as I poured cereal into a bowl.

"He didn't kill anyone," I said, surprised myself that I was defending the man.

Mom walked over and sat down opposite me at the table. "I'm afraid he did," she said softly. "Officer Craig died last night."

I dropped the spoon I had been holding.

"Oh, Emmy Lu," Mom said, "did you know Officer Craig well?"

I didn't say anything. I just sat there watching the cereal get all soft and mushy. *T.J.!* I thought suddenly. I had to talk to T.J.

"What time is it?" I said, jumping up.

"Almost ten," Mom said.

"I have to go."

"But you haven't eaten."

"I'm not hungry. This is terrible."

JEAN Blasiar

My mom nodded, came over to me, and put her arm around my shoulder. I let her believe that the reason I was so upset was because Officer Craig was a friend. Actually, I didn't even know him.

Mom was playing with my frayed pigtails. "Maybe you shouldn't ride your bike around town today," she said unexpectedly. What made that occur to her, I wondered.

"Why?" I asked.

"They haven't caught that man yet. I have kind of a creepy feeling."

"Oh, Mom. He's probably out of town by now."

"We could use today to shop for new school clothes."

I just looked at her. What an awful waste of a beautiful summer day. "You pick up something," I suggested, and I meant it. "I hate doing that."

"Emmy Lu, look at you. You're at least an inch taller than last spring. I can't buy skirts and pants without you. They have to be hemmed."

"Aw...Mom. Not today. I promised T.J."

She seemed to be softening. "Absolutely then, tomorrow we go shopping. We can't wait any longer. School starts next week."

She was kidding. "You're kidding."

"I'm not. Look at the calendar. It's the end of August."

Where did it go? Three months. "I have to go," I said more urgently than ever.

After I dressed and was headed out the door, Mom called me back. She wouldn't *not* let me go. She wouldn't.

She stuffed a five-dollar bill in my hand.

"What's this?"

"Get something to eat."

"Five dollars?"

"Treat what's his name."

"T.J.? T.J., Mom. Tommy John Blake. Not what's his name."

"T.J. He seems like a nice boy. Too bad he's going to Franklin."

"*WHAT?* You, too? I'm glad he's not going to my school."

Mother looked surprised. "Why?" she asked.

I winked as I shoved the five in my pocket and picked up my bike lock. "We both play first base," I said. "Thanks for the money."

Still, she called to me before I left the driveway. "Don't make any plans for tomorrow."

Tomorrow. I would try not to think about it. Maybe it would never come. Shopping! How I hate shopping. "Take this off. Put this on. Stand still while she pins, Emmy Lu. Did I stick you, dear?"

What was it I was so anxious about this morning before shopping popped up, I wondered. "Oh…" I said out loud as I turned the corner of Circle Drive. "Officer Craig."

JEAN Blasiar

T.J. was sitting on the lawn in front of the courthouse reading a newspaper when I arrived. He looked up when he heard my brakes squeak.

"Did you hear?" he asked first thing.

I nodded, got off my bike. "Is it in the paper?"

T.J. showed me a picture of Officer Craig, whom I recognized, and another picture of two men.

"Are those the guys they captured?"

T.J. nodded.

"Is one of them the guy you said you'd recognize?"

He shook his head.

"T.J.!" I knelt down on the grass beside him. "You mean the guy you got a look at is…is… "

"The killer," T.J. said, pointing to the paper. "There's kind of a description of him. I'm sure it's the man I saw kicking the tire."

"And you don't know if he saw you or not?"

T.J. held his head. "He might have," he admitted. "He looked at me at the window. It's possible, if the sun wasn't in his eyes."

I closed my eyes and tried to picture that train in the cornfield. "Let's see, we were going east and it was early…" I opened my eyes; afraid to say what both of us knew.

"The sun was behind him," T.J. said stiffly. He punched me in the shoulder playfully. "Good thing you had that cap on."

Suddenly, sitting right out there on the courthouse lawn where anyone walking by could see didn't seem like a smart idea. "Let's go someplace," I suggested.

"The pond?"

"No!"

"Why not?"

"Because it's dark and it's hidden and nobody goes there anymore but you and me."

"So?"

I tapped the newspaper. "That guy's hiding somewhere. Maybe. Maybe…"

"Maybe what?"

I got back on my bike and motioned for T.J. to follow me. "Maybe he hitched a ride out of town, and is long gone," I said cheerfully, reassuringly. I didn't believe it myself, but I hoped it was true.

T.J. was slow to get on his bike. He tucked the newspaper into the space under his seat. "The police are watching all the roads out of town," he said, without looking at me.

"He could still get away," I said hopefully. "I'll bet he's in…Pittsburgh by now."

T.J. had been looking very grim. His face broke into a welcome little smile.

"HEY!" I shouted, remembering. "I've got five dollars. I'll buy you lunch."

"I haven't had breakfast yet."

"Good idea. Breakfast. Come on."

We had the diner pretty much to ourselves. I walked to the back booth purposely so we could talk and not be overheard.

T.J. ordered a sweet roll. I had the works—pancakes and bacon and syrup.

"And hot chocolate," I added, handing the waitress the menu. "T.J.?"

He looked up at me. "What?"

"Hot chocolate?"

"Oh. Yes. No. Yes."

The waitress looked at him once more, but he nodded. "Yes."

Maybe food, I thought, would bring him back.

"You know, Em," he said softly, turning his knife over and over again and staring at it, "if I hadn't spiked those tires, Officer Craig would still be alive."

I leaned over as far as I could across the table between us.

"What are you saying?" I whispered. "What's that got to do with anything? You helped the police, even if they don't know it. If it hadn't been for you…"

"If it hadn't been for me, Officer Craig would still be alive."

"And those three guys would have taken off with everything. They'd have gotten away with it."

"But Officer Craig would still be alive."

I couldn't get through to him.

"Stop it!" I murmured sharply. "*YOU* are not to blame! They had guns. They might have shot anybody who got in their way. They might have shot you or me or both of us. You're a hero, even if we can't talk about it."

"I'm not."

"You are, and I'm not listening to any more!"

The waitress brought our order. T.J. didn't say anything for a very long time. I ate some bacon and one pancake.

"Eat your sweet roll," I urged. "Have one of these pancakes." But he just sat there, turning and staring at that knife beside his plate.

I wasn't going to say any more about it. I decided just to try to get him involved in something else, even the raft if it took that, but he wouldn't drop it.

"They'd have gotten away with all the money and the jewelry and the other stuff," he said.

He was beginning to worry me the way he sat there and repeated himself over and over again.

"But nobody would be dead."

"T.J.!" I said sharply. "Stop it! What can you do about it? Nothing."

That's when he looked up at me and said, "I think we have to tell someone, Em."

I about died right there. "You don't mean it!" I cried softly. "You can't be serious."

50

JEAN Blasiar

"I am."

He looked serious. "Who do you want to tell?"

"Mike Evans."

"Who?" The name didn't mean a thing to me.

"Mike Evans, the reporter for the *Chronicle*."

"*A REPORTER?* Are you crazy?"

"I'm not, Em. Mike Evans came over to our house last night."

I knew it! I knew something had happened between the time he left me yesterday at my house and this morning. He was different. He'd been so hopeful yesterday that the police would catch the man who got away, and now he was willing to run to a reporter, of all people, and tell him the whole story.

"Mike's been dating my mother," T.J. was saying. He had me so upset I could hardly follow him. "He talked about nothing else last night but the robbery."

"At your house?"

T.J. nodded. "He came for dinner. That's when he talked about the whole thing."

"Did you say anything to him? T.J....you didn't!"

But he shook his head. "No."

I sighed. A big sigh.

"I wanted to talk to you first." He leaned over and looked me right in the eye. "Em...I want you to go with me to his office."

"No! Absolutely not. Un-uh."

"Don't say no. Listen to me, and don't say anything until I finish. Promise?"

I didn't promise.

"They don't have a very good description of this guy they're looking for. He wore a mask when he robbed the train, and no one on the train gave the police a very good description. But when I saw him, Em, out that back window, he wasn't wearing a mask. I SAW his face. I know exactly what he looks like. Exactly."

He wasn't convincing me.

"I have to tell the police what I know, Em," he said. "And if I do, then I have to tell them the whole story of how and why we were there."

I shook my head. "NO!"

"Just listen, Em," he pleaded. He was definite. His grip on my hand was very firm. "I think we can trust Mike Evans. If we talk to him, he can tell us what we should do. Maybe he'll go with us to the police."

"How do you know we can trust him?"

"I said I think we can."

"He's only after a story."

"And my mother."

"T.J.!"

He relaxed his grip on my hand. "They really like each other," he said. "I could tell the way they looked at each

JEAN Blasiar

other during dinner. He made a couple of phone calls to his editor and the police, but he stayed at our house until after midnight. He and my mom sat on the porch swing. I could hear them talking."

"So? That doesn't mean anything."

"It means that he's going to try to help his girlfriend's son. He won't do anything we don't want him to."

I put my head in my hands. He was confusing me. I never in the world dreamed that I would have to tell anyone about yesterday. Not even my mother. Especially not my mother! Thank God my father was out of town. It was the first time that summer I was grateful for that.

"Em," T.J. said, "you don't have to go with me. I can tell Mike that I was alone in that car. Nobody saw us. He'll never know otherwise."

"Absolutely not!"

"Why not? There's no reason to involve you."

"I *am* involved."

"You don't have to be."

I stared at him. I have a very wide stubborn streak to match my very red hair.

"I'm going with you," I said, then slumped back in the booth. If I didn't know that T.J. Blake was not a devious rascal, I'd think I'd been led into that trap blindfolded. Especially when I noticed how he perked up after I agreed to go with him.

"You'll be glad, Em," he said cheerfully. "You'll really be glad when you meet Mike. Pass me one of those pancakes."

Reluctantly, I followed T.J. on my bike to the *Chronicle*. For me, this trip was worse than a visit to the dentist, worse even than shopping for new school clothes, which tops my hate list. But there was no stopping the determined, sandy-haired boy in blue jeans and yellow shirt who stood waiting for me to lock my bike in front of the *Chronicle*.

It was useless to argue with him anymore. Once he walked through those tall glass doors, our secret would be out.

Mike Evans was in a meeting.

"Let's come back later," I whispered excitedly to T.J., but he said, "We'll wait!" to the receptionist, took my arm firmly, and led me over to some chairs.

It's probably a fascinating place, the *Chronicle*. I sat on a very uncomfortable chair and watched a woman type and another one file. *The newsroom must be on another floor*, I thought. It must have been a very busy place yesterday, with the robbery and all. But today, it was a tomb.

I was getting that same sick feeling I had the day before, but I knew that if I got up to leave, T.J. would stay right where he was, waiting to see Mike Evans.

He was a rascal, I decided. He knew I wouldn't let him go through this alone. The only good thought I had was that if I'd been the one who wanted to tell somebody, even the police, T.J. would have gone with me, I'm sure.

I glanced at him, but he was staring at the wall. *He's probably getting his story together*, I thought. "Our" story together.

A man in his mid-thirties, kind of short, nice black hair, good-looking actually, wearing a tweed jacket and dark pants, came walking down the hall and stopped when he saw us.

"Tommy?" he said.

"Mike," T.J. said, standing. "I wonder if we could see you a minute? This is Emmy Budd."

I smiled.

"Emmy," Mike said, shaking hands with me. "Sure thing. Come into my office."

We followed him, Tommy first, me a very unwilling second. How do you know if you can trust a person you've never met before, I wondered. T.J. had been so sure.

I sat down in the chair next to T.J. Mike Evans leaned against the front of his desk and faced both of us. The door to his office was closed.

"What's up?" he asked. He seemed friendly. I liked his face. "Would you like me to show you around?" Naturally, he would think that's why we were there.

T.J. shook his head. I tucked my hands under my legs

to keep from biting my nails, which I do when I am very, very nervous.

Mike looked at T.J., then at me, then back at T.J., waiting.

"We...uh..." Tommy began. "We have a story to tell you, Mike, but first, we'd like you to promise that you won't repeat it to anyone unless we say it's okay."

Mike folded his arms and stared at T.J. He seemed mildly interested, I'd say, not bored, not fascinated, but mildly interested.

"Okay," he said. *He'll probably regret agreeing to that*, I thought, as T.J. squirmed in his chair.

"It's about the robbery," he said.

Mike's eyes closed a little. I never took my eyes off his face. I knew that I was going to be able to tell something about him by watching his reaction to what T.J. was about to tell him.

"What do you think happened to the getaway car?" T.J. asked.

That was a good start. I approved of that. Find out what he knew first, before we gave it all away.

Mike scratched his face. "Well," he said, "as far as anyone knows, somebody tampered with the tires."

"Who?"

Mike refolded his arms. I could tell by the way he settled back against the desk that he was interested now.

He shook his head. "Nobody knows," he said. "The police thought that maybe some workers in the field might have found the car and slashed the tires as a prank."

T.J. looked at Mike. He didn't say anything right away. I began to wonder if he had changed his mind about telling the story when I heard him say, "Maybe it wasn't a prank. Maybe someone stopped the robbers from getting away."

Mike Evans seemed very interested now, the way his jaw set, and his eyes stared. You can learn a lot by watching a person's face when they hear a story for the first time, especially when you know what's coming.

"That is possible, I suppose," he admitted.

"It's more than that," T.J. said quickly. "It's what happened."

Mike nodded his head slowly. "You seem to know a lot about it, Tommy," he remarked.

T.J. glanced at me. I smiled, and it was all the encouragement he needed to go on.

"We were there," he said bravely. "Emmy and I were the ones who slashed the tires. Actually, Emmy watched so I could do it without getting caught."

Mike looked at me. His jaw hung very loose now, his mouth open. He looked back at T.J.

"How?" he said, his surprise showing on his face.

"We were hiding in the baggage car," T.J. confessed.

"When the train stopped, we saw two men get out of a black car and walk up to the train. They had shotguns. One of them had an axe."

"And you…?"

"And Emmy and I ran into the cornfield. While Emmy watched, I pounded spikes into the back tires. Then we ran back to the baggage car."

"What were you doing in the baggage car?"

"We were going to Pittsburgh."

Mike smiled, just a little around the corners of his mouth. If I hadn't been watching his face so closely, I may not have seen it.

"Pittsburgh?" he said.

I laughed. It was funny the way he said it.

"You crazy kids." I think he really was shocked. "You might have been killed," he said.

We both nodded. Later, that had occurred to both of us also.

"Your mother doesn't know?" Mike said to T.J.

T.J. shook his head.

Mike looked at me and I shook my head also.

"Nobody knows?"

We both shook our heads.

Mike started to walk around his desk. Then he turned and looked at T.J. "Did you see the men?" he asked.

T.J. said, "A little."

"Have you seen the paper this morning?"

"Yes," T.J. said.

"Is there anything that you can tell us about the man who got away? We don't have very much to go on."

"We?" T.J. asked.

"The police. I'm covering the story for the *Chronicle* and the wire services. The police have let me in on everything they have. There isn't much of a description of the killer."

That word sent chills down my legs. I tightened my grip on the chair.

"The only one who really could describe the man for us, or pick him out of a mug shot, is Officer Craig."

T.J. shifted in his chair.

"One witness said the killer was wearing a mask," Mike went on. "And another one said he was wearing dark glasses. No one can describe him."

Mike was waiting for T.J. to say something. He looked at T.J. anxiously when he spoke. "We know his approximate age, height, and weight, but that could fit a thousand men."

T.J. finally admitted, "I did see the man who got away. I watched him out the back window of the baggage car. He wasn't wearing a mask then."

Mike turned to face me. "Did you see him too, Emmy?"

I hesitated. "Not very well," I said. "Only his back. I was too scared to watch."

Mike nodded. "I can believe you were scared," he said.

I liked him. I liked Mike Evans. He could believe that I was scared. I felt a lot better about him. T.J. had been right to want to go to Mike if we had to tell anyone, which I wasn't altogether certain about yet.

"You have anything to say, Tommy?" Mike said. "Anything at all you can remember that might help identify him?"

T.J. fidgeted. "Well," he said, "the only thing I remember was how mad he was at the car. He kept kicking the wheel and kicking it, time after time, hard as he could. I don't know how he could stand it without breaking his foot. I thought he was…"

"Crazy," I piped up. "That's what you said when you were watching him. You said, 'He's a crazy man, Em.'"

It came back to me suddenly. I startled myself by speaking up, but T.J. agreed with me.

"That's right," he said confidently. "I remember that now. I remember saying he was a crazy man. Not that he was acting crazy. Of course, he'd be furious when they couldn't get the car turned around, but the fact that he stood there kicking that wheel, beating the heck out of his foot like that."

Mike studied T.J.'s face.

"Don't you think that was kind of stupid, Mike?" T.J. asked. "I mean, were these guys experienced? They did some pretty stupid things. Why wouldn't they have turned that car around, heading in the other direction *BEFORE* they robbed the train? Why lose time after the robbery turning around or backing up in a cornfield?"

Mike continued to stare at T.J. All three of us were thinking about what T.J. had said, I guess. I know I was. T.J. hadn't mentioned that to me before, but it certainly made sense. I wondered if it puzzled him all the time, or if he just thought of it that minute.

"Good thought," Mike said admiringly. I could tell that he liked T.J. "This was a first robbery for two of them anyway, the two who are locked up. We think the third man was the leader. They're all very young, about twenty-five." He started pacing again in front of his desk.

"What you said, Tommy," he went on, "about the guy kicking the wheel. How many times did you see him do that?"

T.J. shrugged. "I don't know," he said, "eight, ten, twelve maybe. He just kept it up like a madman, which I guess he was."

"But he would have busted his foot if he kicked that wheel as hard as you say he did that many times."

"You'd think so," T.J. said.

Mike sat down on his desk again. "Well," he said, "now we start looking for a man with an injured foot. Sometimes the body can stand more than we think it can when we're under a lot of pressure, or angry as this guy was, but later, later the body hurts just the same." Mike shook his head. "Nobody mentioned this guy having a limp or anything. The two guys in jail aren't talking, period. There was so much confusion at the station yesterday, I wonder if anyone would have even noticed a limp."

"I'll bet it's worse than a limp," T.J. remarked. "I'll bet he broke his foot."

Mike put his hands in his pants pockets. "I'll check it out," he said. He looked at both of us. "Is there any chance that this killer got a look at either one of you?"

T.J. looked at me and I said, "Go ahead, tell him."

"Did he, Tommy?" Mike asked quickly.

"I don't know," T.J. said. "He looked at the back window, right at me, one time, but I don't know if he saw me or not."

Mike now had that same worried expression that I must have had when T.J. told me the same thing the first time. "You, Emmy?" Mike asked.

I shook my head. "No," I said. "I'm sure."

Mike smiled. "Not even those pigtails," he said.

"I was wearing a cap," I replied, embarrassed to admit it.

But Mike only chuckled. "Okay," he said, straightening up. "I want you off the streets, Tommy. Go home and stay there. I don't care what excuse you have to make to your mother. Tell her you're not feeling well. Get in your house and stay there. If this guy is as crazy as you say, and right now he is a hunted, wounded animal, he is extremely dangerous. And armed. He knows you can identify him. We have to hope he can't identify you."

My legs were shaking.

"If I take you home," Mike said to T.J., "it just might make somebody suspicious. Everybody in town knows I'm working on this case. They stop me wherever I go and ask about it."

T.J. nodded.

"How did you get here?" Mike asked.

"My bike," T.J. said. "It's downstairs."

"You, Emmy?"

"Same," I said.

Mike took each of our hands and we stood up. "Okay," he said, "I'm grateful that you came to me with this story. Thank you for trusting me. I promise you I won't tell anyone. If I did, your lives might be in real danger." He looked at each of us hard again. "You're sure you didn't tell anyone else?"

We both said definitely that we hadn't.

"Good," Mike said. "Very good. I'll keep in touch with you."

He put a hand on T.J.'s shoulders. "I'll call you at home later this afternoon," he said to T.J. "I hope you understand that I don't think you should tell your mother about this. It would just make her nervous and she'd want to stay home with you and that would certainly alert anyone who was hanging around The Chili Bowl. The fewer people who know the story the better. Okay?"

T.J. nodded. "I don't want to tell her anyway," he admitted.

"I hope you won't have to," Mike said. "Okay, Emmy?"

"You bet," I said. "I didn't even want to tell you."

He put his arm around me. "I'm glad Tommy convinced you," he said. "It was a very brave thing for both of you to do."

"Sneaking on the train?" I said. "Or telling you about it?"

Mike laughed. "Both," he said. "Especially brave of you to come here and tell me about it."

He walked to the door with us. "Pittsburgh?" he whispered, making us laugh once more before we left.

I did. I liked Mike Evans.

T.J. and I said good-bye downstairs. I watched him ride west toward his house, and I headed east. I could have amused myself downtown, I guess, or gone over to Debbie's house, or swimming, but nothing interested me. I felt lost without T.J. There was an emptiness that I wouldn't have been able to explain to anyone.

I rode my bike home and parked it in the garage. For me, the summer and the vacation were over.

Eight

I could easily have spent that afternoon alone—would have preferred it, actually—but when I walked in the back door Mother said, "Debbie phoned. She wants you to call her back."

I made a face.

"Did you get something to eat?" Mother asked.

"Oh…yeah." I reached into my jeans pocket. "Here's your change."

"That's all right. Keep it."

I didn't argue. "T.J. went home," I said. "He wasn't…feeling very well." And that probably was very true. "I'll call Debbie."

Already I missed T.J.; I missed him very much. The thought of doing something with Debbie again…gad! T.J. and I had been together every day for…how long had it been? Weeks anyway. Since the third of July, actually. That morning I sloshed my pigtail in my ice cream. I'd never forget it.

Debbie answered on the first ring. "Hi," I said. "What's up?"

JEAN Blasiar

"I am *BORED!*" she screamed into the phone. "I want to do something!"

"What?" I asked.

"Anything." She didn't care. She just wanted to do something. "How about going to the malt shop?" she suggested.

The malt shop? Gad! "In August?" I said. "Everybody's gone."

"Yeah," she agreed. "Boy, is it ever Dullsville around here. I hate summer. I wish school would start."

I groaned.

"Well, don't you?" she shouted through the phone. Then she added quickly, "Oh, no, of course, you don't. You and that cornball you run around with are having a great summer. Just how far have you gone with this guy anyway?"

"Shut up!" I said.

Mom shot me a look and a sharp, "Emmy Lu!" from across the kitchen.

I put my hand over the phone. "She bugs me," I whispered.

"That's no reason to be rude," Mom said. She then left the kitchen, probably because she didn't want to hear, and I tried once again to be friendly.

"Well?" I heard her say more than once.

"Well, what?"

"Let's do something! I am bored out of my mind sitting around here."

"Okay," I said, giving in. "Want to go bowling?"

"No," she said flatly. "I hate bowling."

I waited.

"Let's go to a movie," she suggested.

"What movie?"

"What difference does it make? Anything is better than sitting around watching these cornball game shows on television."

Cornball. That was Debbie's new word.

"I'll check the paper," I suggested.

"Don't bother. My mom said she'd take us downtown. We can see whatever's playing while she shops. Or we can look around for new school clothes. What do you think?"

"The movie." Anything was better than shopping for new clothes. Besides, I still had to do that with my mother tomorrow. I shuddered at the thought of it. Another day I wouldn't see T.J.

"Pick you up in fifteen minutes," Debbie was saying. "What are you wearing?"

"Jeans."

"You would be. Why don't we wear shorts? Never can tell who we might run into downtown."

"You wear shorts. I'm wearing jeans."

JEAN Blasiar

"If you'd wear something other than jeans all the time you'd attract a better class of boys."

"*FIFTEEN MINUTES,*" I said sharply and hung up.

Gad! I had really outgrown Debbie Farwell that summer, or she had outgrown me. I preferred to think that I had outgrown her.

With Mrs. Farwell in the front seat of the car, Debbie didn't mouth off about my jeans or T.J. or anything.

The movies downtown were nothing. One of them I thought I could have sat through, but it was rated "G" and Debbie wouldn't be caught dead standing in line for it.

"So what are we going to do for a couple of hours while your mother shops?" I asked disgustedly. Coming downtown was a real dumb idea; I was beginning to think.

"Don't sweat it," Debbie said. "There's lots to do."

"What?"

"We can spend an hour or more in the record store."

"Gad!"

"Oh, come on, little girl, grow up. Listen to the beat and maybe you'll get with it. Take a look around at the guys inside. See what you've been missing."

I started to follow her into the record store reluctantly.

"Hey, Emmy," Debbie said suddenly, grabbing my arm and jerking me around, "is that your dad?"

"WHAT? WHERE?"

I turned around so quickly that I knocked Debbie's purse off her shoulder.

"Watch it, dope!"

"Where? Where do you see him?"

"Oh…I guess not," Debbie said casually. She never did point out the man she saw. "It sure looked like him, but it isn't."

I didn't believe that she saw anyone at all who resembled my dad. I swear she did that on purpose.

"Is he still out of town?" she asked casually, which is what she really wanted to know.

"Yes," I said, hoping that would end it.

"Where?"

"California."

"Oh, really. Why didn't you go with him? Wouldn't you just love to see California?"

"No," I lied. "Let's get a drink. I'm dying."

"If he's in California, why did you turn around so quickly when I said I thought I saw him?"

"I just did. Drop it."

"Sure. Only… "

I stopped walking with her. "Only what?" I said. "Get it out, Debbie, and be done with it. Only what?"

"It's just what everybody's been saying, that's all."

I was *FURIOUS*! I was so fuming mad that I knew I was going to do something immature and ridiculous like cry.

"Out with it," I said firmly.

She wanted to tell me. I knew that. How she wanted to tell me. She never saw anyone who looked like my dad at all.

"I just heard from a couple of people that your parents are…separated. That's all."

"*SEPARATED?* Of all the dumb…"

"I'm sorry, Emmy. Your mother being so pretty and all. And your dad. Well, he's so good-looking. I guess all that traveling he does…"

"Will you butt out? They are not separated. Drop it. Tell anyone else who asks you to drop dead!"

"Sure, Emmy. I'm glad to hear it. Of course, you would know."

"You bet I would know. My dad is doing public relations for this publishing company. He's got a lot of work to do in California and other places before he can come home."

"Why didn't you and your mother go with him?"

"It isn't vacation, Debbie. I just told you. It's work."

"Sure. Sure. Let's go get that drink. I don't want you mad at me. I just thought since we were best friends and all, I should tell you."

"Fine. You did. Okay?"

"Sure. Okay."

We walked on toward the hot dog stand. I didn't want

to think about it. I was trying to think kindly toward Debbie. We *had* been best friends. Maybe, just maybe, she had been trying to let me know in her own stupid, bumbling way. I wanted to know who she heard such a thing from, and then again I didn't want to know. Gad! What an awful day it was. Awful!

My eyes burned.

"You know what I need," I said. "I need a pair of sunglasses."

We walked into a little shop and I picked up the first pair of sunglasses I found and put them on. Then Debbie picked up a different pair, took the ones I was wearing off my face, and told me to buy the ones she chose instead. I didn't care what they looked like. When I'm about to cry my eyes get all red-rimmed and, *cheez*, I wasn't going to cry in front of Debbie Farwell. I bought the ones she picked out and we left the shop headed for that drink and then onto the record store.

SEPARATED! What a stupid thing for people to say!

The afternoon dragged by for me, but Debbie was having a ball thumbing through all the records, and I followed her like a puppy. I bought a record because I felt guilty about hanging around the store so long without buying something. Debbie bought five records, not because she felt guilty at all but because she "simply *adores* Elvis..."

JEAN Blasiar

"Come back to my house and we'll listen to them again," she insisted, but I told her I really had a headache, which I did, and thought I better go on home.

Mrs. Farwell let me out in front of my house. I thanked her and told Debbie I'd call her later. I meant, of course, *much* later, like weeks later.

Mom was out in the rose garden when I walked into the kitchen. I saw her through the patio window. There was a message on the desk by the phone. "449-5500." I thought it might be Mike Evans or T.J. or someone from the *Chronicle* trying to reach me, so I dialed the number.

"Athletic Club."

"Pardon me?" I said.

"Athletic Club."

"Oh…I'm sorry. I must have dialed the wrong number."

I sat there listening to the dial tone for a very long time. That terrible word *separated* kept running around in my head. *Separated. Athletic Club.*

One of the boys at school had a father who lived at the Athletic Club. Our team used the pool last fall for practices because the boy's father was a member and a resident. Was Dad…?" The phone rang, and I jumped.

"Em?" the voice on the other end asked timidly.

"T.J.?" I had never heard his voice on the phone before. He sounded so young.

"Can you talk?" he asked.

"Sure," I said quietly. I could still see Mom from the kitchen window. She was very involved with her roses. She looked contented. She didn't look *separated*. "Are you all right?" I asked anxiously.

T.J. said, "Sure."

Sure. The dope. As if he didn't have a thing in the world to worry about.

"I heard from Mike," he said.

"You did? Did he find anything? Have they found him?"

T.J. said, "Sh-h-h. Can anybody else hear you?"

"No."

"Okay. Mike said that he's checking all the doctors and hospitals for a guy with an injured foot, but so far he hasn't turned up anything."

"Oh," I said, trying not to sound too disappointed.

"But he's still checking," T.J. added.

"Good," I said hopefully.

"My mom is due home any minute. I better go. I just thought you'd want to know."

"I did. I mean, I do. I mean, take care of yourself. Stay in the house. Don't answer the door for anybody."

I heard him laugh. "Okay, Sherlock," he said and hung up.

Sherlock and Watson. We really were a pair.

JEAN Blasiar

I felt so much better after I talked to T.J. for those few minutes. I decided to fix myself a bowl of cereal. I was just pouring the milk when Mom came in.

"Before you eat that," she said, "would you like to go out for dinner tonight?" She pulled off her garden gloves. "I hear there's a very good restaurant just opened in the Athletic Club. I was going to call for a reservation."

I nearly dropped the milk. That was twice the same day that I was shocked while fixing cereal, but this was a nice surprise. It wasn't Dad's new residence she had called. It was only a restaurant.

"Yeah?" I said. "Well…you know, I'm really pooped. It's been a long day. Would it be okay if we just had hamburgers or something simple at home?"

I thought she looked a little disappointed.

"Unless you'd rather go out."

"No, not really," she said. "I'm tired myself. I could make homemade pizza."

"Great!"

"And we'll have lunch downtown tomorrow anyway."

"Tomorrow?"

"Emmy Lu! You haven't forgotten! New school clothes?"

I groaned. "Oh…yeah," I said.

"It would help if you'd make a list of the things you want to get."

I carried the full bowl of cereal and milk across the room. "Why don't *you* do that, Mom," I suggested. "You're good at lists."

"But I don't know…"

"Anything," I said. "Anything you want to get." Second thoughts on that. "But no dresses!" I added firmly.

I picked up the record I bought and tucked it under my arm. "Unforgettable" seemed like good listening tonight.

Nine

No matter what the temperature, no matter how many hours the air conditioners run day and night, in our town summer is over the first of September.

Our part of the country tears August off the calendar and immediately gets fall fever. The first of September every year my mom puts her white shoes and straw purses away. Melons and berries suddenly disappear from grocers' shelves. Pumpkins miraculously appear. Cider replaces iced tea in refrigerators. Guys start hanging out at school tossing a football around a week before school opens.

September morn. I wondered where Dad was and what he was doing. *Is it fall in California? Is the air crisp? Is the smell of football and the first frost in the air?* I wanted to ask Mom; *after I go to sleep at night, does he ever call and see how we are?*

Summer, like the train robbery, was yesterday's news. Mike Evans had kept his word. There was nothing in the paper the next morning about two witnesses who had come forth with a description of the...(I hated the word)... killer.

I liked Mike Evans. He was sitting on an exclusive story, but so far he had managed to keep it out of the paper.

Mom and I had breakfast downtown at the diner, the same diner, the same booth even, where twenty-four hours earlier T.J. and I decided to talk to Mike Evans. T.J. had decided. I was trapped.

While we waited for our order to arrive, I took a good look around the diner.

Jerseyville is full of strangers at harvest time. Lots of young men, college age, maybe a little older, working in the fields part time. As young guys walked in and out of the restaurant, I watched closely for anyone with a limp.

"Emmy Lu!" Mother said sharply. "Are you listening to me? How many skirts will you need?"

"What? Oh…one."

"ONE?"

"One skirt, two pairs of jeans."

"Emmy Lu!"

Same argument every year, only this year we were having it at the diner and not at the breakfast table. I think I hate the month of September, especially the first part, and especially this year.

Mom was saying, "I don't suppose you remember that notice the school sent home last June. Girls may wear pants on Fridays *ONLY* this year."

JEAN Blasiar

Gad! I'm pretty good at forgetting things I want to forget.

"What about dresses?" Mom asked. "A shirtwaist, a…"

"NO DRESSES!"

I would *not* wear dresses in seventh grade. You can't do anything in a dress. I'd look like Debbie Farwell in a dress. The coach wouldn't even let me try out.

Our order arrived. Mom waited until the waitress left.

"WHAT are you going to wear to school?" she said sharply. Already she was getting angry and we hadn't even started shopping. It was bound to get worse.

"Okay. Two skirts," I conceded.

"What about the other days?"

"I'll wear each skirt twice."

Mom was staring at me.

"I'm saving you money," I argued, taking a big bite of waffle. Mom put her list back in her purse and ate her waffle in silence. We were just about finished when she said, "You're going to need a new winter coat."

"Mom," I said in a calm voice, "no coat, huh? How about a jacket? An army jacket. We can go to the army surplus store on Sixth Street."

Mom put her fork down and I knew I was in for it. "You're almost thirteen," she reminded me. "WHEN are you going to start dressing like a young lady?"

"Mom…I don't want to try on coats on a day like this.

79

Let's wait till it gets cold. Maybe it won't get cold this year." Fat chance.

We ate the rest of our breakfast in silence.

Mary Anne's Store for Young Girls opened at ten. We were there at five after. A fat saleslady in a tight dress with purple eye shadow came up to us eagerly. She gave me a very pathetic look. In less than two minutes she and my mother had an armful of clothes ready for me to try on. Mom waved for me to follow her into the dressing room. I smiled at Purple Eyes as she started to follow us in also.

"We can manage," I said in the sweet voice I use for such people. "We'll call you if we need help."

She looked so-o disappointed. "I'll be right out here, honey bun," she gushed. "Wouldn't you like a pair of stockings and a little heel to try on the pretty things?"

I grinned and shook my head, hoping Mom hadn't heard.

Inside the dressing room, Mom had hung four skirts, two jumpers, and a dress.

"Where are the jeans?" I whispered, but she ignored me.

"I'm not sure I have the right sizes here," she said, holding up one of the skirts. It was plaid. Plaid!

I shook my head. "No plaids!"

She held up a green one and a red one and I shook my head again.

JEAN Blasiar

"This pretty blue one?"

I didn't know how many more I could turn down before she'd really get angry. "Any denim?" I asked hopefully.

"EMMY LU!"

"Debbie has a denim skirt. Everyone does." That might have been stretching it just a bit.

Mom held up the jumpers. "I hate jumpers," I said. "It takes too long to get into gym clothes."

"Well? What then?" Mom said, quite a little annoyed.

"Blouses," I said. "Get some blouses. We can get jeans and a denim skirt at a place I know in the square."

Mom picked up all the skirts, the two jumpers, and a horrible-looking dress that even she didn't suggest I try on. Purple Eyes must have selected that one. Mom walked out, leaving me alone in the dressing room.

While I was rearranging straight pins in a little red pincushion on the table, our saleslady stuck her head in.

"How are we doing in here, lovey?" she purred. She looked around the empty room. "Where are your lovely things?" she asked.

"I…I'm just getting over chicken pox," I said. "I can't try on anything because I have this greasy ointment all over my back. Have you had chicken pox by the way?"

Purple Eyes backed out the door, not even a friendly, "I'll be back, lovey," as she left.

Mom came in with four blouses. I tried them on over my sleeveless shirt. Two I hated. One wasn't too bad, and the last one was cute.

"A plain white blouse, Emmy Lu?" Mom said when I handed her the one I liked.

"Okay," I said. "This one, too." It was pink. It had sleeves that I could roll up and a collar that I could unbutton. It looked like a boy's shirt. The more I studied it, the more I liked it.

Mom looked at it a long time. "I guess," she said, hesitating. She held it up to me and looked in the mirror. "Yes, it sets off your hair nicely. Some shades of pink on redheads…" she murmured.

"Those two, Mom. Let's go."

"But the skirts?"

"Not here. There's a pants store in the square. I can get jeans and a denim skirt there. It's a neat place."

The way she picked up the blouses and headed out, I knew she'd given in. It wasn't such a terrific battle after all.

I hung around the desk, making our saleslady extremely nervous as Mom wrote a check for the blouses. Just when I thought the saleslady was going to suggest that I look at one more thing, I scratched a couple of times, and she moved ever so slightly away.

We found the skirt I was talking about in the little shop

on the square. The jeans needed washing four or five times, but there was still time before school started.

We went to another store to buy socks and underwear. Mom hesitated at the bra department, but I took her hand and moved her right along.

Instead of the jacket I wanted, we compromised on a raincoat with a heavy liner and two bulky sweaters. I did very well, considering. Nothing in the bunch that I absolutely hated getting out of bed in the morning to put on.

It was almost noon by the time we finished. I suggested that we stop and have a quick bite at this new little outdoor café on the square. I ordered French fries and a soda, but Mom also told the waiter to bring me a hamburger. She had the fruit salad. She always has the fruit salad. In summer. In winter, she has the spinach salad. I think it must be very boring to be a grown-up.

"Looks good," I said when the waiter brought our order. I was starved now that the shopping was over, and eager to eat. Between bites I watched the young men who walked by the café. *THAT* was the real reason I wanted to eat outdoors. And yet, I didn't have a clue about the guy I was looking for.

"What kind of shoes are you going to get?" Mom asked. I thought the shopping was over. Shoes?

"Shoes? Tennis shoes. What else?"

Mom was shaking her head. "You didn't read that note from school."

"No tennis shoes? What is this?"

"Only on…"

I stopped her. "I know. Only on Fridays. Gad! How am I going to live until Fridays?"

"A little heel, maybe?"

I think she had heard that saleslady. A heel! In junior high! Gad!

"Let's go to McMillan's," Mom suggested.

We weren't finished. I wasn't so sure that there wasn't going to be something about our purchases yet that I hated.

We drove two blocks to the shoe store, not that we couldn't have walked. It was a nice day, but Mom wanted to put the packages in the car.

Mr. McMillan was very patient. He brought out every color oxford shoe he had in my size—brown and white, blue and white, black and white, even white and white.

"It's the white part I don't like," I admitted finally. "It's so…white."

While I was trying to decide, a man came in and walked to the back of the store, where Mr. McMillan also repaired shoes. Mom was busy looking at something in the window.

JEAN Blasiar

"Walk around in those shoes, Emmy," Mr. McMillan suggested, "while I help that young man in the back."

I did get up and walk around. I walked to the back of the store when I heard the young man Mr. McMillan was waiting on say, "Can you re-stitch this for me while I wait?"

I just happened to glance his way as he took off his shoe, and then I saw it. He had no toes on one foot! He was a young man, about twenty-five.

ABOUT TWENTY-FIVE?

I stared at the shoe he handed Mr. McMillan. Where the stitching was torn a steel plate was exposed. *STEEL!*

Kicking and kicking and kicking that wheel like a crazy man.

I took a good long look at him, trying hard to remember everything about him—what he was wearing, what color his hair was, how long his hair was. He wore dark glasses. Couldn't see his eyes. Long, pointed nose. Hair over his ears. Hairy arms. Some kind of big ring on his right hand. Big hands.

I had to call Mike!

"I have to go," I whispered hurriedly to Mom.

"Go? Where? What about the shoes?"

"I don't know."

I couldn't wait until Mr. McMillan wrote up the sale

and Mom made out a check and on and on. He might get away. I had to call Mike.

"I have to check with Debbie first about the color," I lied to Mom. "I don't know which one everyone's wearing."

"Get the color you want," Mom said.

"I have to go!" I insisted.

Mom said softly, "To the bathroom?"

"Yes." I was afraid she was going to ask Mr. McMillan if I could use his. "And the library," I added quickly. "I just remembered there's a book I have to read this summer for English class."

"EMMY LU!"

Gad! She said my name right out loud like that!

"Do you mean to tell me that you have a report due and you waited until one week before school starts to read the book?"

What if it *was* him and he had seen me looking out that baggage car window even if I was wearing a cap? Mom was certainly drawing attention to me.

I took the oxfords off quickly and jammed my feet into my old tennies. The more I tried to remember what that man in the cornfield looked like, the more certain I was that this was the guy.

"Where will you go to the bathroom?" Mom whispered. "Maybe Mr. McMillan…"

JEAN Blasiar

"NO! I can make it to the library. I'll get my book," I said quickly, "and maybe I'll come back here or go someplace else and try on more shoes. You go on home, Mom. Have a nap or something. I'll call you later and maybe you can pick me up."

I didn't give her a chance to argue with me. She knows better than to argue with me when I have to go to the bathroom. I always wait till the last minute. I almost talked myself into the idea that I really did have to go. I took Mom's arm and led her to the door.

"We're going to think about the shoes, Mr. McMillan," I called, my back to the two men in the rear of the store. I rushed Mom out so fast that her purse caught in the door.

"Emmy Lu, watch what you're doing!"

"Sorry," I said, opening the door and closing it again. Mom's car was right in front of McMillan's.

"Thanks a lot for the clothes, Mom, and breakfast and lunch."

"You call me later when you want me to pick you up," she said. "See if you can reach Debbie by phone at the library and maybe she can come down and look around with you."

Oh, wonderful! "Sure, Mom," I said, closing the car door and waving.

I glanced quickly into the shoe store to make certain

that the man with the steel shoe was still waiting, and then I ran as fast as I could down the street and around the corner. I stopped at the phone booth outside the drugstore.

"Please be in! Please be in!" I said over and over again while I looked up the *Chronicle* number in the book. The first time I dialed wrong and had to press down the bar and start over. Making a phone call can take forever when you're frantic.

Nothing seems to work. I have this nightmare all the time about trying to get a phone call through when I'm in trouble and I can't. This was it—my wide-awake nightmare.

Finally, I heard a woman say, "Mr. Evans' office."

"May I speak to him, please. It's Emmy Budd calling."

"I'm sorry," the woman said. "Mr. Evans is out of the office right now."

"Terrific."

"I beg your pardon?"

"Nothing. When will he be back? It's an emergency."

"Well," she said, "I might be able to reach him if you want to leave a message."

"I do. Would you tell him to meet me as soon as possible—like in the next ten minutes? I'm at the drugstore on the square."

"Does Mr. Evans know you, Miss Budd?"

JEAN Blasiar

"You bet," I said. "Tell him that, please. It's a matter of life and death. At the drugstore, as soon as he can." I hung up before she had a chance to say anything else.

And then I waited and waited, pacing up and down outside the drugstore. I couldn't leave to see if the guy was still in McMillan's or I'd miss Mike.

About twenty minutes after I spoke to his secretary, a car pulled up in front of the drugstore and Mike Evans opened the door and motioned for me to get in.

"Hurry," I said, slamming the door after me. "Around the corner, McMillan's Shoe Store."

"Emmy," Mike said, "what is it?"

"There's a guy in there," I said. I was so out of breath—probably from being nervous. My heart was beating a thousand times a minute. "In the shoe store, McMillan's Shoe Store. Drive there."

"What guy?"

"A guy with half a foot. Three-quarters, maybe." I sat on my own feet, turning to face Mike. "Mike," I said, "he has a steel plate in his shoe. Steel!"

The car braked suddenly. Mike looked at me. "How do you know?" he said.

"I saw it!" I cried. "I was in McMillan's trying on new school shoes with my mother and this guy came in and asked Mr. McMillan if he could re-stitch his shoe while he waited."

Mike parked about half a block from McMillan's. "Duck down," he said to me.

"But, Mike… "

"Down!" He pushed me down gently. "This guy you saw has also seen you, my dear," he said. "You aren't exactly a nondescript person."

"What does that mean?" It was hot on the floor of Mike's car and I wanted to see.

"Your pigtails," Mike said. "Stay down now. If he sees you pointing him out to me, there could be trouble. Even Mr. McMillan might be in danger."

"Well, don't just sit there," I argued. "Go on in and see if he's there. I'll stay down. I promise."

"You're sure?"

"Yes. Please go," I cried. "I know it's him."

Mike opened his door and I heard him walk down the street. It was almost as hot, scrunched down on the floor of the front seat of his car, as it had been under that tarp in the baggage car.

Despite the predicament I was in, I smiled. "It isn't very comfortable, is it?" I said to myself, remembering. That described my summer very well—uncomfortable. But fun.

Mike was back in five minutes. I couldn't wait for him to close the door.

"Well?" I said.

"Gone." He sighed. "No sign of him."

"Oh! Did you ask Mr. McMillan about him?"

"No, I didn't. I can't make anybody suspicious, Emmy. And I certainly can't involve you."

"Let's drive around," I suggested. "Maybe I can spot him."

Mike wasn't starting the car. "I'll drive a few blocks, and then you can get up," he said. "I'm not going to search for this guy with you in the car. It's too dangerous."

"But I'm the only one who can recognize him."

Mike started driving. "Did you get a good look?"

"Yes. I really did. I tried to remember everything about him. I hope I don't forget anything."

"Let's go to Tommy's house," Mike said. "His mother's working this morning. We can talk there." Mike turned a corner and motioned for me to get up.

"If you and Tommy can agree on a description of the man," Mike said, "then we'll really have something to go on."

I was watching everything, every store, every street we crossed, every alley for some sign of the man with the steel shoe. Mike parked at the curb and stopped. There was a phone booth on the corner.

"I told Tommy not to answer the door for anyone," he said. "I better call him and tell him we'll be there in a few minutes."

While Mike called T.J., I watched everything that

passed—cars, trucks, pedestrians. It was true. There was a killer walking the streets of Jerseyville and I was probably the only person in town besides T.J. who knew who he was.

T.J. was so glad to see us. "Hi! What's up?" he asked eagerly when he opened the door.

It was a nice house. It wasn't huge or anything, but it was nicely decorated. Mike and I followed T.J. through the front hall into the living room, where T.J. told us to make ourselves comfortable.

Pretty wallpaper in the living room, a thin blue stripe. The sofa was blue velvet. One chair was a green print and the other a blue print. I sat in the chair with the blue print. I was so anxious to tell T.J. about the man I saw, but I took a second to look around the comfortable-looking room and tell T.J. how much I liked his house. It looked like him. And it looked like his mom. I wondered how a boy who liked to do such uncomfortable things like riding rafts and boxcars could live in such comfortable surroundings. There was a piano in the corner.

"Who plays?" I asked, nodding toward it.

"My mom," T.J. said abruptly. "Will you tell me? I'm dying."

I grinned. "I saw him!" I blurted out.

T.J.'s eyes bulged. "WHAT?" he said. "But how did you recognize him? I thought you didn't get a good look at him."

JEAN Blasiar

"I didn't."

"Then how do you know it was him?"

I told T.J. the story of what had happened in McMillan's. He listened without saying a word. So did Mike.

"You think it's him?" T.J. said excitedly to Mike when I finished.

Mike reached into his inside jacket pocket and pulled out a notepad and a pencil. "That's what we're here to find out," he said.

He turned to me. "What color hair, Emmy?"

"Brown," I said.

Mike and I both looked at T.J. and he nodded.

It was exciting. I could hardly stand it. Like at the end of the Sherlock Holmes movies just before he points out the killer. I love that part.

"Long? Short? Curly? Straight?"

"Long," I said. "You know." I put my hand to my collar. "About here, and it covered his ears. Curly. No, wait. Wavy. Hairy arms and a big ring on his right hand. Very large hands, hairy fingers. Let's see…he was wearing some kind of dark blue work pants and a striped shirt, also dark." I closed my eyes and tried to picture him again. "What did I forget? His nose. A long, pointed nose, big lips. Not a very attractive man. I couldn't tell anything about his eyes. He wore sunglasses."

"Even in the store?" Mike asked.

"Yes. He didn't take them off while I was there."

Mike and I both looked at T.J. "Well?" I said. "Is that the same man you saw?"

T.J. seemed a little unsure. "I guess it could be," he said. "He was wearing something dark. When he turned around I got a good look at his face. He did have a long nose; I remember that. Don't remember the lips. Hair was the way Emmy described it. Heavy black shoes."

"Yes! Heavy black shoes!" I cried. "How many young guys wear that kind of shoe? They're one of a kind, I'll bet. Specially made with that steel toe. The stitching came loose because of the way he kicked that tire. It's him. I know it's him."

Mike looked at T.J., then back at me. He wrote down everything we said.

"You think it's him now, don't you, Mike?" I asked.

Mike nodded slowly. He looked over his notes. "I do," he said finally. "It just seems like too much of a coincidence. The steel shoe explains it all."

"Oh, T.J.," I cried. "We found him!"

"*YOU* found him, Emmy. Wasn't it lucky you went shopping today."

"Yeah," I said. "Imagine shopping being lucky."

Mike stood up. "I'll take you home, Emmy," he said. "And then I'm going to ask a guy I know at police headquarters to draw a picture of the man you just described." He tucked his notepad and pencil back into his jacket pocket. "We can still make the morning paper if we hurry. I don't know what my editor is going to say when I tell him what I want to do."

"Do you have to go, too," T.J. said to me.

I nodded. I didn't want to, but I knew I should. I would have liked to hang around, have T.J. show me the rest of the house and the yard. Maybe shoot a few baskets with him.

"I have to go to the library," I said. "I told my mom that I had to read a book before school starts. It was the only way I could get rid of her. She's going to pick me up later."

T.J. laughed. "Now you're stuck reading a book, genius," he said. I made a face at him.

"Okay, Emmy," Mike said, "let's go. I'll drop you off at the library on my way to police headquarters. Lock the door behind us, Tommy."

I really hated leaving. First of all, I would have loved doing something again with T.J. It seemed like such a long time since we had talked. What was it, two days? And second, we knew for certain now that the guy who killed Officer Craig was still hanging around town. I was scared for T.J.

At the library I picked up the first skinny book I found.

Did you ever wake up early and lie there trying to identify sounds? I did that the next morning. The barooooomph was the water heater. The barroom barroom was the air conditioner in my mother's room. Not my mother's room. My PARENTS' room!

There was a sahwish, sahwish outside that I decided was a rainbird in our neighbor's front yard, and a hummmmmmmmmm that must have been a plane, and the clip-clip, clip-clip, turn, clip-clip, clip-clip of a mower. I had them all figured out by the time I heard a ploppppppppp at the front gate. The morning paper had arrived.

Very carefully, I sneaked down the steps without waking Mom. Thank you, Mr. Edison, or whoever, for noisy air-conditioning.

I also managed to open the front door without it creaking—the first time I can ever remember—and run barefoot quietly down the walk in my nightgown, without anyone seeing me. Another lucky day, I hoped.

The door clicked louder than I expected it to, but not loud enough to waken Mom. I tiptoed into the kitchen and opened the paper on the table.

JEAN Blasiar

If we didn't have this anti-shock juice running through our veins, sudden jolts like the one I got when I opened the paper and saw the picture of the man in the shoe store staring at me could be fatal. The artist had captured him perfectly. It was definitely him. I wondered if Mr. McMillan would open his paper and recognize the man whose shoe he repaired. It also occurred to me that my mother just might recognize him, also. What if she remembered where she'd seen him and what happened after that?

I folded the paper in half, hiding the picture. After I poured myself a glass of milk, I settled down to read the article by Mike Evans.

It was a thrill seeing Mike's name in print. Also realizing that "two passengers on The Commodore the day of the robbery have come to this reporter and given the above composite drawing of the killer" were, in fact, me and T.J.

While I was sitting there devouring every word, the phone rang. I spilled the milk getting to the phone on the first ring.

"Hello," I whispered into the phone.

"Emmy, this is Mike," the voice said.

"Oh, Mike!" I was so relieved. For one crazy, terrifying moment, I thought it might be "him," the guy with the steel shoe, calling. But how absurd!

"Good news, Emmy," Mike was saying. "A foreman on a farm outside town called the paper. I talked to him a few minutes ago. He said he saw the picture in the paper this morning and he's sure that it's the same guy who's been working for him a couple of days."

"REALLY?" I shouted, forgetting about Mom.

"The police are on their way out there now. I'll call you back when they get in with the suspect."

"Okay! Don't forget to call me."

Mike laughed. "How could I do a thing like that," he said. "Stay cool."

I held the phone, listening to the hummmmmmmmm on the other end. It was a wonderful morning for sounds. Another lucky day.

I never left the kitchen that morning. It was after one before Mike called back and I was still in my nightgown, sitting at the table, watching a portable TV, one eye on my mom in the rose garden and one eye on the TV for bulletins.

"Emmy," Mike said excitedly. "I think we've got him. He has a steel plate in his right shoe. You were right."

"ALL RIGHT!" I cried. "Can T.J. leave the house now?"

Mike didn't say anything for a few seconds.

"Mike," I said. "You there?"

"Yes," he replied. "Emmy, I have to bring Tommy down here to identify this man."

"What about me? I helped identify him, too."

"I know, honey, but you can't actually point him out as the one who robbed the train. You admitted that you didn't get a good look at him. But Tommy did. Right now he's our only witness."

"But, Mike…"

"Sorry, Emmy, but Tommy is going to have to be the one to identify him. I'm working now on the details of how I can get him in and out of police headquarters without disclosing his identity."

"Please, Mike, let me come, too. Maybe I'll remember something important. I was there. I'm a witness too, right?"

He didn't say anything.

"Please, Mike," I pleaded. "I promise I won't get in the way."

"You wouldn't be in the way," Mike said. "I'll have to make the same arrangements for one as I would for two witnesses, I guess."

"Then it's okay?"

"Can you come down to the police station without telling your mother? I hate to ask you to do that."

"Sure I can."

"Well…let's see, it's one ten. How about two o'clock? No…wait, Emmy. Come to the *Chronicle*. I'll have to get both of you in the police station and out without anyone seeing you…somehow. I'll worry about that. You come to my office at two. Can you make that?"

"You bet."

I was changed, on my bike, and waving good-bye to my mom before one-thirty. Nothing could have kept me away. Gad, what an exciting day!

I almost didn't get to go. Mom made me promise that I would read every afternoon for the next week, or until I finished my library book and report. I told her, "It's a skinny little book." I couldn't remember the title. Something like *A Pitcher in the Rye*, or something like that. Probably very boring, but I knew I could finish it by next week.

Crazy title for a book, I thought, as I pulled out of the driveway and headed for the square.

Eleven

T.J. and I were scrunched down in the back seat of Mike's car, a blanket over us, trying hard not to giggle at every bump in the road or at just anything at all.

I whispered once, "It isn't very comfortable, is it?" and got T.J.'s fist in my back.

"Quiet, you two," Mike said. "We're here."

He turned off the ignition.

"Stay where you are, under that blanket, and be quiet until I tell you to come out."

"It's dark," I whispered.

"We're in the underground parking lot of the police station," Mike explained. "I've parked right next to the door to the witness room, but first I want to make sure that the instructions I left have been carried out. Don't get out of the car. I'll be right back."

We didn't say a word while he was gone. We really didn't. I guess T.J. was as nervous as I was. On the other side of the door out there was a killer waiting to be identified, and T.J. was going to have to do it.

It wasn't very long before Mike came back.

"Okay," he said. He opened the back door of the car.

"You can come out now. Everyone is staying out of the area where we'll be."

"But, Mike," T.J. said as we unfolded legs and arms and tumbled out of the back seat, "how are we going to identify him for the police if they can't see us?"

"You'll see," Mike said. "And remember, *YOU* are the one who is doing the identifying, Tommy. Not Emmy. You are not to consult with her about your decision. If you decide this isn't the man you saw rob the train, say so. Or if you're not sure, tell us that also. You understand that?"

T.J. nodded.

"Emmy?"

I nodded. "I won't say anything," I assured him.

"Okay, let's go. They're waiting for us."

I walked behind T.J. I decided not to be seen and not to be heard. I was the invisible Emmy Budd—a spook.

Mike led the way down a narrow hall and into the first room. We all went in. It was a small room with a large drape covering one wall. T.J. and I sat down.

"Face the drape," Mike said. "Now, Tommy, I'm going to turn off the light and open the drape. There are four men on a stage in the next room, facing us. Behind this drape is a very large window. We can see the four men, but they can't see us. There's a police officer in the room with the men. Several policemen are in the line up in street clothes along with the suspect. Don't be frightened. No one can see us and no one will hear what we're saying in here until I turn on this microphone." He showed us a small hand gadget. "Take your time. All the time you need. And don't say anything unless you're absolutely certain. Okay?"

T.J. nodded. Mike looked at me and put a finger to his lips. Then he turned

off the light and opened the drape.

At first, we didn't see anything, but a bright spotlight went on in the next room. Four men were lined up on a stage, just as Mike had said. A policeman was sitting on a stool talking over a microphone to the men on the stage.

Mike switched his microphone on. "Okay, Mac," he said. "We're ready."

"Right, Mike," the officer said. There were marks on the wall behind the four men. Three feet, then inch marks, four feet, inch marks, five feet, inch marks, six feet, inch marks. No criminals over seven feet, I guess.

The policeman at the microphone asked the men on the stage to face the right side of the room. One man turned the wrong way.

"Right side," the policeman said again, and they all faced right. They stood there a few seconds.

"And now the left side, please," the policeman said, and they turned left.

"Face the back of the stage, please," he directed them, and then, "and now the front again, please."

T.J. was staring at the stage. Mike leaned over and whispered, "You can talk, Tommy. Only the officer at the microphone can hear you through his earphones. No one else in that room can hear you."

Mike glanced up at the four men and switched on his microphone.

"Is there anyone on the stage, Tommy, that you can say positively was the man you saw rob The Commodore?"

T.J. pointed to one of the men. "The second man from the right side," he said.

The officer in the other room asked the man T.J. pointed out to step forward two steps.

Mike looked at T.J. He switched on his microphone again.

"Is that the man you saw at the scene of the robbery?" he asked.

"Yes, it is," T.J. said distinctly.

Mike looked at me and I nodded. It was him.

"Okay, Mike," we heard the officer say. "The man up front will remain in custody. Everyone else may go."

Mike drew the drape. We left as quickly and as quietly as we had arrived, back into the car and under the blanket. Mike started the ignition, and it was all over.

I was shaking under the blanket. T.J. had just condemned a man to a prison sentence, or worse maybe, now that Officer Craig had died. I couldn't help thinking, what if we hadn't hidden in that baggage car that morning? What if we hadn't told Mike about it? What if I hadn't shopped for new shoes yesterday?

"What happens now?" T.J. asked from under the blanket.

Mike waited to answer until he stopped the car. "Come up for air," he said. "Let's get a drink."

We were parked in front of the diner.

"This okay," Mike asked, "or would you like to go to The Chili Bowl and tell your mother the whole story?"

"WHAT?" T.J. cried. "Are you joking?"

Mike held open the door of the diner and we walked in. We walked to the back, to that same booth where T.J. and I had breakfast the morning he convinced me to go see Mike Evans, the same booth where Mother and I had sat discussing new clothes.

T.J. and I sat on one side of the booth, Mike on the other.

"I wonder if we should tell your mother," Mike said calmly. "I'm afraid you might have to be a witness for the state when this man is prosecuted."

"Oh, no!" T.J. cried. "You mean in court? In front of everybody?"

"Listen, Tommy...Emmy...it may be necessary to tell

the whole story in order to get a conviction." He wasn't smiling. T.J. and I were both slumped down in our side of the booth.

Mike ordered three large sodas when the waitress came. T.J. and I remained silent.

After the waitress left, Mike said, "The railroad will probably thank you. Maybe even reward you for your part in the capture of these guys."

T.J. looked over at me and then at Mike. "You said it *may* be necessary to tell the whole story. Maybe not?"

Mike let out a big sigh. "If we can get a confession out of this guy, or if either of the other two starts talking and implicates the others, there won't be a trial."

The waitress brought our drinks.

"Let's see how it goes," Mike said. "Drink up. We won't tell anyone yet. There's a chance that we won't have to tell anyone *ever*." He smiled. "Of course, if you're interested in any reward…"

"Forget it!" T.J. said. I agreed.

Mike drank some more and then excused himself to get back to the office. He said he'd call T.J. later.

I waited until Mike paid the check, waved to us, and left the diner before I asked T.J. what he thought.

"Were you scared?" I asked.

"You mean this morning?"

"Then," I said. "And now."

"I wasn't then, not even at the police station, but I am now." He shook his head. "I don't mind too much if I have to tell my mom," he admitted. "I don't want to and I sure hope I don't have to, but with Mike there it won't be so bad. The part that really scares me is that court-room."

"Me too," I admitted.

"Imagine all those people there we know. And having to look right at that man and say, 'He's the one.'"

T.J. looked straight at me. "Your part in all this would have to come out, too, wouldn't it?" he said sadly.

I nodded. "I guess so," I said.

"We could just tell them that I was alone in the baggage car."

"Hey," I said, "we've been through that already, remember? Besides, it isn't honest. You'd be under oath, you know."

"Yeah," T.J. said, hanging his head. "I guess." He sighed. "I'm really sorry, Em, that I got you into this mess."

"That's okay, Ollie," I said playfully, scratching the top of my head, but T.J. didn't even smile. "Let's go to a movie or something," I said. He had me almost crying.

We walked from the diner to the *Chronicle* to get our bikes. After we unlocked the bikes, T.J. looked at me and said, "I don't really feel like going to a movie, do you?"

"Sure, I do," I lied. "There's a horror movie at the State. Come on. I feel like letting out a good scream."

"Oh…okay. I have to stop by The Chili Bowl and get some money from Mom."

"I've got money. I still have change from that five dollars and I've got some other money that I took shopping."

T.J. hesitated. "I can get some," he said.

"What? Won't let a girl pay for the movie? Since when?"

He smiled, just a little, but I was relieved to see it. I got on my bike and started on ahead. He followed. I wanted to tell him that I liked it much better when he led.

It was a hot afternoon, no matter what the calendar said. Maybe air-conditioning, a box of popcorn, and a cold drink would pick us up again, I hoped. Wasn't I bursting with excitement that morning? What was I so happy about and what was so different now, I wondered. The police had the killer. T.J. could feel safe again. And we might *not* have to go to court, Mike said.

I was hoping for the scariest movie I ever saw in my life and I would scream and scream and scream, but as it turned out the movie didn't scare either one of us very much. I don't know if T.J. had his mind on it at all. I know I didn't. I kept thinking about a courtroom with a judge and a jury and my mother sitting in the front row and T.J. and me at a table with Mike and an attorney, and

JEAN Blasiar

T.J.'s mother sitting next to my mother, and Debbie Farwell in short shorts whispering to all my friends behind my back, and Mr. McMillan and the widow of Officer Craig, and policemen and the man with no toes looking right at us when we pointed him out.

It gave me the creeps. It was creepier than the *Creature from the Swamp* on the big screen.

When the movie was over and the cartoon started, T.J. whispered, "Want to go?"

I didn't, but I said I did. It was still hot and still sunny outside. I'd lost track of time.

"What time is it?" I asked T.J.

He looked around for a clock. "Five-thirty," he said.

"I guess I better go home."

"Yeah, me too. Thanks for the movie."

I hated that, him thanking me for the movie. "See you tomorrow," I said. "I'm glad you can leave the house again."

He smiled. "Yeah," he said, "me too."

I wanted to say something to cheer him up, so what did I say but, "School will be starting soon." Gad! What a dumb thing to say.

"Football," I added. "Volleyball."

"Baseball," he said. There was still some life in him.

"Right," I said cheerfully. "Next spring." So far away. Next summer was even farther.

The sun was just going down. The temperature dropped five degrees while we were standing there.

"There's a nice breeze," I remarked.

T.J. didn't notice. He was looking around like he wanted to go. The first time I ever felt that he wanted to go when he was with me. Summer and the things we did together were definitely over. I knew I was going to cry. How I wished I had my sunglasses.

I waved without looking back as we took off in opposite directions.

That's the way it's going to be from now on, I realized as I headed slowly down Main Street. School. Debbie. And those people Debbie said were talking about me and about my parents. Already people whispering behind my back. Wait till they found out about stowing away on The Commodore.

The papers would carry all of it. *TWO KIDS AND A REPORTER TRACK DOWN KILLER!* Even Mike wouldn't be able to keep that out of the paper. What if the wire services picked it up and carried it all the way to California? Pictures. Pictures of T.J. and me and The Commodore. Emmy Budd, Most Valuable Player. Emmy Budd, runaway. Emmy Budd, hobo.

As I rode home that afternoon, I realized, probably as T.J. had realized, that I had to tell my mother everything. Everything. And I had to convince her that we *were* planning on coming back to Jerseyville that same day. We weren't running away. Not her daughter, too.

Would it be better, I wondered, to get Mrs. Blake and my mother together, and T.J., Mike, and I could tell them at the same time? My eyes were burning, my head ached, and I rode right through a stop sign.

Almost immediately a horn beeped behind me. I pulled up to the curb, expecting a black-and-white patrol car to pull up beside me. Now I was going to have a ticket to explain as well. For a day that started off great, this one was sure winding up a disaster.

The black-and-white car turned out to be a green sedan. Mike was driving and T.J. was sitting in the front seat next to him.

I was shocked. I started to say, "I thought you were…"

T.J. laughed at me. "You thought we were the police," he said. "You know you went through a stop sign, Miss Budd."

"What are you doing here?" I said, brushing away some water on my cheek.

"I thought you had to get home."

"I thought you did."

"I'm going."

"At a snail's pace."

"Well…I'm not anxious."

Mike leaned over T.J. "I've been looking all over town

for you two," he said. "I found Tommy on his way home. Get in."

"My bike…"

"Leave it. I just want to talk to you a minute. I'll pull up."

It was so unexpected. I had this big lump in my throat. T.J. didn't look at all like the boy I left almost half an hour ago. He was smiling and laughing and what all.

"Wait till you hear," he said excitedly as I got in the backseat. He had turned around and was facing me.

"Hear what?" I said nervously. "I hope it's good news. I don't think I can stand any more bad news today."

"Tell her, Mike."

Mike turned around to face me. It was hot in the car. I was perspiring. I think that was perspiration on my cheeks.

"Well…*TELL ME!*" I cried.

Mike said, "I wanted to tell you earlier today, when we were having that drink at the diner, but I wasn't sure yet. That's why I left you to go back to the police station and find out for sure."

"WHAT?"

"The knife wound that Officer Craig received wasn't deep enough to kill him. We knew that, but we kept it out of the papers until after the autopsy. Anyway, the coroner called in the autopsy report a little while ago. Officer Craig died of a heart attack."

I looked at T.J. That was it? So…T.J. didn't have to feel

guilty anymore about causing Officer Craig's death. Of course, that was good news.

"Tell her the rest," T.J. said, grinning.

"When the man Tommy pointed out in the lineup was told that the officer he stabbed didn't die from the wound but from a heart attack, he pleaded guilty to a lesser charge of armed robbery and assault."

"Emmy! Did you hear what Mike said? The guy confessed. There won't be a trial. We don't have to tell anybody anything."

I was going to cry. I knew I was going to cry. My throat was tight, my eyes burned, and that wasn't perspiration on my cheek. I was already bubbling over. Why oh why didn't I think to bring those danged sunglasses?

"Emmy!" T.J. shouted. "I thought you'd be jumping up and down all over the place."

Mike put his hand on my arm. "You've had a very nervous day, Emmy," he said tenderly. I know he knew I was going to cry. "Go on home," he said. "Do you want me to put your bike in the trunk and drive you home?"

I shook my head.

"We'll celebrate tomorrow," Mike said. "I'll take you both to lunch."

"I have to read tomorrow," I said stupidly, my dumb voice cracking in the middle of it. And what a stupid thing to say at a time like this. Read! Gad!

But Mike looked at me understandingly. "How about this?" he said. "I'll call your mom and ask if you can go with Tommy and Tommy's mother and me to the State Fair on Saturday. How's that? It's on the *Chronicle*."

I smiled as much as I dared. "Great," I said carefully. Then I got out of the car. There was so much I wanted to say—thank Mike, thank T.J., thank everybody—but I couldn't open my mouth. My chin was quivering. It always does that when I'm about to cry. I must have looked a sight.

Mike started the car.

"Don't go through any more stop signs," T.J. said softly, and winked.

I didn't look back after I got on my bike, but I waved. As they passed me, I heard T.J. say, "Take care, Budd. See you Saturday."

It wasn't *Pitcher in the Rye*. It was *Catcher in the Rye*, and it's no little girl's book. I finished it in one afternoon and the next day I decided to go back to the library and see what else that guy wrote.

Mike called. He talked to my mother. He's so good at explaining things that there wasn't any problem about my going with them to the fair.

"Seems like a nice young man," Mother said after she hung up.

"Un-huh," I agreed. I really didn't want to discuss Mike in too much detail, how well I knew him, where I met him, that kind of stuff. I just let Mom believe that he was T.J.'s friend and, of course, his mother's.

"He's a reporter?"

"Yep."

"For the *Chronicle*?"

"Yep."

"And he's dating T.J.'s mother?"

"Right."

"He asked if I'd like to go along."

"Oh?" I didn't know he was going to do that. "Would you?" I asked.

"No," she said. "But it was very nice of him to ask."

"Why don't you go?"

"Not this time," she said.

I was sitting at the breakfast table reading Mike's column about the robbery and the arrest.

"Did you finish your book?" Mom asked. She was having a cup of coffee at the table while I read the paper.

"Yes," I said. "I'm going to take it back to the library today. And I think I'll go get those shoes at McMillan's."

"Which ones?"

"The blue and white ones. They'll go with my jeans and that blue denim skirt, I guess."

Mother sipped her coffee. "Did you read in the paper about how Mr. McMillan waited on that man they arrested?"

I stared at the paper. "Really?" I said.

"We were in there that same day," Mom said. "It's such a coincidence."

"What is?"

"Oh, our being in McMillan's and Mike Evans writing that article for the paper. I guess…I guess it's just that Jerseyville is really a very small town."

"It certainly is," I agreed.

"And I suppose people gossip a lot, too. Don't they?"

JEAN Blasiar

Was it getting sticky, or was I imagining it? I didn't say anything. I picked up the paper and my bowl of cereal and took them over to the sink.

"Do you like Jerseyville?" Mom said unexpectedly.

I set the cereal bowl down, tucked the paper under my arm, and headed for the hallway. "I guess," I said. "I guess I do."

"You have lots of friends."

"Well, not lots, but good friends. I like the school."

She was leaning against the counter. I was getting really nervous about what she was trying to say.

"It is a nice town," she said. "Next year I think I'll join the PTA and try to get more involved."

"Good idea," I said. What *had* started all of this thinking? Maybe it was learning that T.J.'s mother was dating Mike Evans. Suddenly my own mother wanted to get out and meet more people, "get more involved", she'd said.

"I may take a course at the university."

That was really shocking. She'd never talked about doing things like that before.

Mom looked very pretty standing there in her peach dressing gown, her auburn hair just brushing the collar of her robe. A very pretty lady, if I had to say so myself. Maybe someday, I hoped, I'd look like her. She wouldn't have any trouble meeting people—meeting men—if that's what she wanted to do. I shuddered at the thought.

117

I guess T.J. was used to having his mother date. I knew I'd never get used to it.

"I'm sorry we didn't do anything this summer," she said apologetically. "But with your father being away so much... "

"That's okay," I said quickly. "I like it here. I had a good summer. We didn't have to go anywhere."

"Do you like it as much as the desert?"

Ah-ha! A trap! If I said, "No," then maybe she'd consider moving back to Arizona. If I said, "Yes," then maybe we'd never see Dad again, if that's where Dad was. It was close to California, and he always liked the desert. Something had made her bring up the desert.

"I like them both," I said, chickening out. "I love the snow. I'd miss that if we went back to Arizona. I like the change of season. Don't you?"

She looked at me curiously. "I think...I think I like it here very much," she said surprisingly. "I'm going to make it a point to get to know our neighbors and the people at the church and at your school better. I think we should entertain more, have a few parties for some of your friends and their parents. I'd like to meet them. Maybe we should invite T.J. and his mother and Mike Evans for dinner one evening. Would you like that?"

"Sure," I said. "I'll introduce you when they pick me up tomorrow."

JEAN Blasiar

She was smiling. "Good," she said. "I have some new recipes I want to work on before we invite them. It'll be fun."

I walked over and kissed her on the cheek. I was so glad that I didn't have to tell her a very scary story, even if it did have a happy ending.

It had been my plan to ride my bike to the library and the shoe store later, but with Mom in such a melancholy mood, I asked instead if she would drive me.

We didn't do much except stop for a triple treat sundae after our shopping, but I enjoyed it. I think she did, too. It reminded me that we used to go as a family to the ice cream parlor after dinner. I hoped it didn't remind her as well.

While we were sitting in the ice cream store eating our sundaes, Mom suggested that maybe I should have a couple of inches or more cut off my hair.

"Just the split ends, Emmy Lu," she said.

I groaned.

"If you don't want to, all right."

"Oh...I don't know. I was going to wash it tonight."

"They'll wash it. Maybe you'd even like to try a new style."

"No!"

She nodded.

"Just a couple of inches?"

Unfortunately, when we stopped at the beauty salon, they had someone who could take us right away. Mom said as long as she was there she might as well have hers done also. Somehow, I got the feeling that I'd been trapped into the whole thing, that it was what my mother had planned for the day—a trip to the beauty parlor for me. I might not have been surprised to find out that we both had appointments. She can be very clever.

When the girl was brushing my hair, she asked me how I wanted to wear it.

"In braids again, please," I said, but she kept curling it over her hand, and when she finished she had me take a good look at it, front and back.

I smiled. "In two braids, please," I said, handing her my rubber bands.

She leaned over and whispered, "If I let you walk out of here in braids, I could lose my job. I'm supposed to make you look different than you did when you came in, right?"

"Wrong."

"Then you go home and put it in braids, but when you walk out that door you are going to look different. Did you see the back?"

"Yes."

"And the side?"

"Okay," I said. "Just leave it. I'll braid it myself when I get home."

JEAN Blasiar

"Emmy Lu," Mom said, coming up to my chair, "your hair looks lovely."

I grinned at my mom in the mirror. "Can we go?" I whispered when the girl went to get change. "I hate the smells in this place."

"You really ought to wear your hair that way," Mom said again.

I took another good look in the mirror before I took the bib from around my neck. Debbie Farwell would have loved my hair. When I leaned over it fell in my eyes. Gad! I picked up my rubber bands, thanked the gal who "did" me, and we left.

In the car on the way home, I braided it again. Mom shook her head and sighed.

When we got home I went up to my room and tried on the new denim skirt with the pink shirt and the blue and white oxfords. Probably, Mrs. Blake would wear a dress to the fair, I thought. I took a good look at myself in the full-length mirror, then took off the skirt and hung it up; I took out my old jeans and my tennies and laid them on the other bed for the next day. I also laid out the pink blouse with the jeans. *That* I would wear. It didn't matter what Mrs. Blake wore. I was going to feel like myself.

The next morning when T.J. rang our bell, I was waiting.

"Mom!" I called upstairs. "They're here."

"Hi," I said to T.J. "I want my mom to meet your mom and Mike."

"Okay," T.J. said. He leaned against our door. "Pretty blouse." He'd never said anything about my clothes before.

"Thanks." I was really surprised.

Mom joined us. "You remember T.J.," I said.

"How are you, Mrs. Budd?"

"Just fine, T.J., thank you. Looks like a great day for the fair."

T.J. agreed that it was.

As we walked out to the driveway, Mike got out of the car. He was wearing jeans and a plaid shirt, and I thought he looked much younger than he did in a coat and tie.

"This is Mike Evans, Mom," I said, "and T.J.'s mother, Mrs. Blake."

Everyone exchanged hellos and "isn't it a beautiful day for the fair" and "I hope it won't be too crowded today." That stuff. Mike asked my mom again if she was sure she didn't want to come along.

"Plenty of room," he said, smiling at her warmly.

When I looked into the car, I didn't think it was all that roomy. Two in the front seat and two in the back was about all it could hold. I also noticed that Mrs. Blake didn't insist that Mom join us. T.J.'s mother was friendly and that was about it.

JEAN Blasiar

"Emmy Lu and I want the three of you to come to dinner some evening soon," Mom said as T.J. and I got in the backseat. "Emmy Lu, do you want a sweater?"

"No, thanks." I hate "Emmy Lu." T.J. nudged me in the ribs.

Mom waved good-bye and Mike got in and started the car.

"How are you, Mike? Mrs. Blake?" I asked as we backed out.

Mrs. Blake turned around and smiled at me. "You know, Emmy," she said, "we're going to have to do something about names. *Mike and Mrs. Blake* makes me feel like Mike's mother. Why don't you call me Aunt Jane or something? Even 'Jane' if you like. Would that be all right?"

Was something sticky? "Sure," I said. "Aunt...Jane." I wondered if I'd ever get used to that. Maybe, I thought, after I got to know her a little better, I might try just "Jane."

When we were on our way, I leaned over and whispered to T.J., "If Mike marries Aunt Jane, will I call him Uncle Mike?"

I got a fist in my side. I have more bruised ribs since meeting Tommy John Blake.

"Are you ready and anxious for school to start, Emmy?" Mrs. Blake asked. "Is it Emmy, or Emmy Lu?"

T.J. snickered.

"It's Emmy, and no, I am not."

"Not ready or not anxious?"

"Neither one. I'd like another six months of summer."

She turned around to look at me. "Don't you get a little bored with hot weather though?"

"No, ma'am."

"Not at all?"

"No, ma'am. It's been a wonderful summer." I smiled, looking straight ahead, not especially at the back of Mike's head and very especially not at T.J.

"I love summer, too," Jane Blake said, "but come September I really get kind of itchy for fall clothes and wood-burning fires and snow."

"I like the fires and the snow," I said. "If we didn't have to go to school, I'd like it even better."

"Oh, it's school you don't like."

"Yes, ma'am."

"Well, you have lots of activities in junior high. Will you try out for the girls' volleyball team?"

I hesitated. "If I don't make the boys'," I said, waiting to see how that went over.

T.J. looked at me, like I was sure he would. He laughed. I'm sure he thought I was kidding. Mike laughed. Only Mrs. Blake didn't laugh.

JEAN Blasiar

"That's a lovely shade of pink you're wearing, dear," she said. "You redheads look so great in pink."

WE redheads! Mom had been wearing pink. Mrs. Blake turned around to face the front and that was the last thing she said to me all the way to the fairgrounds. I decided that I definitely noticed a change in her just since she met my mom. *WE* redheads!

It took almost an hour to drive to the fair. Mike and Jane talked in the front seat. T.J. and I played two-thirds of a ghost in the back. T.J. won. I think that was the game I was supposed to win. Girls win at spelling games, boys at sports. Something like that.

"Let's play something else," I said.

"Do you like cotton candy, Emmy?" Mike asked.

"Love it."

T.J. whispered, "You can get it all over your face. You redheads look so great in pink."

I grinned at him. "You're cute," I said. "I'll bet nobody's ever told you that before."

He grabbed my pigtail. He let go when Mike announced, "We're here."

The last time we heard Mike say, "We're here," we were scrunched down in the backseat with a blanket thrown over us. I looked at T.J. and he smiled. I knew he was remembering the same thing. Our secret. I hoped neither

T.J. nor Mike ever let Jane in on it. No one had to know now, not Mrs. Blake, not my mother, not Debbie, not the California papers, or even the Arizona papers…if that's where he was.

As she got out of the car, I realized that Jane Blake was really a very pretty lady, maybe not as pretty as my mom, but pretty still. She had light brown hair, like T.J., and she was very tan. Good figure. They looked good together, she and Mike.

I was glad, when I saw how far we had to walk to the main gate, that I'd worn jeans and tennis shoes. Jane also wore pants. I'd really figured her for a skirt. She was such a skirt kind of woman, but that's probably because I'd only seen her at The Chili Bowl, where she always wore a uniform. I noticed as she walked ahead with Mike that she had a very tiny waist. Maybe even a little slimmer than my mom. Maybe.

Mike and T.J. stood in line at the gate for tickets. Jane and I moved over to one side.

"How do you know Mike so well, Emmy?" Jane asked me suddenly.

My father says that I am very good at "bending the truth." It does help, in spots like this especially.

"I want to be a reporter some day," I lied. "I hang around the *Chronicle* a lot."

JEAN Blasiar

"Oh?" Jane said. "I didn't know you were interested in journalism."

"Yes, ma'am," I said.

"Well," Jane said, "both Mike and Tommy are very fond of you. Sorry your mother couldn't join us today."

There it was. "It was really nice of Mike to invite her," I said. "But she couldn't have come. She's expecting a call from my father."

Jane said, "Is he coming home?"

"Of course," I said quickly. "As soon as he finishes this merger he's putting together. He's in California, you know."

Jane smiled a little. "I heard he was out west," she said.

I wondered who she heard that from and where "out west."

"California," I repeated.

Jane was looking at me sympathetically. "I suppose you miss him very much," she said.

"Yes, I do," I admitted, this time truthfully. "We're very close. The family, I mean."

She did a strange thing then. She put her arm around me. "That's wonderful, Emmy," she said. "I know a child misses his father very much." She did say "his," and I didn't correct her.

I discovered once again that I liked her. Back at our

house and in the car I think she must have felt a bit threatened by two more women friendly to Mike (and I include myself in the "women"). There was no reason for me to compare Jane Blake and my mom. My mom is happily married and I am very happy about that.

When Mike and T.J. came back with the tickets, T.J. mentioned to his mother that a neighbor of theirs was standing in line. The two of them walked over to talk to the woman. I grabbed the opportunity to speak to Mike alone.

"Mike," I said quickly, "if Mrs. Blake asks, I've been seeing so much of you because I want to be a reporter. I've been hanging around the *Chronicle* a lot. Okay?"

Mike handed me a book of tickets. "And I thought you just liked older men."

He had a cute smile. I resisted giving him a big hug. What would Jane have thought of that?

"You kids want to go off by yourselves and meet us someplace for lunch?" Mike suggested when T.J. and his mother rejoined us.

I was all for that. Surprisingly, so was Jane. Maybe not so surprisingly. It was obvious how much she enjoyed being with Mike.

"Want to meet at that revolving restaurant at twelve?" Jane asked. She pointed to a big donut-shaped tower in the middle of the fairgrounds. "I hear the food is pretty good."

JEAN Blasiar

"Does it revolve while you're eating?" I asked.

Jane laughed. "Emmy Budd," she said teasingly, "don't tell me the little girl who invented the MT Special has a nervous stomach? I won't believe it."

She didn't have to say "little girl." T.J. yanked on one of my pigtails. "Come on, little girl," he said, "I'll beat you at target shooting."

Jane and Mike wandered off by themselves. The target-shooting T.J. wanted to try was a duck shoot—little plastic ducks moving along a conveyor belt in a big pool of water. Fifteen shots for a dollar. T.J. gave the guy running the booth a blue ticket, and the guy gave T.J. a gun. Fifteen shots later, the guy had fifteen downed ducks.

"Pick your doll," the guy shouted to the crowd.

T.J. looked over the selection. "The one with red hair," he said, pointing to the top row. The guy brought down a Kewpie doll with red hair and blue glittery eyes and handed it to T.J., who then handed it to me. "Should have green eyes and a pink shirt," he said proudly.

"Where'd you learn to shoot like that?" I said, taking the doll.

"A couple of years ago," T.J. said, "we lived in Illinois about a mile from the fairgrounds. I went to the fair every day for three weeks and shot ducks."

"Oh," I said. "I suppose you gave away lots of Kewpie dolls, too."

T.J. leaned over, yanked on my earlobe, and whispered, "My mom has a drawer full of 'em."

I didn't care how many Mrs. Blake had. The one with the red hair was mine.

I was about to suggest that I try my luck at shooting ducks, but T.J. suggested instead that we try the baseball throw.

In the baseball throw there were categories for different age levels. Every hour a prize was awarded to the person in that age group who threw the fastest ball.

When we got to the booth the best time posted in the boys age level ten to thirteen was forty-five miles an hour.

"Is that fast?" I asked. I didn't know anything about it.

T.J. said, "Are you kidding?" He picked up the baseball. "That's really fast," he said, but he decided to try it anyway. I watched him loosen up.

I couldn't help noticing that the fastest speed that hour for the girls in the same age group was thirty-five miles per hour. Thirty-five didn't seem that fast to me.

T.J. wound up and let her rip. His speed went up in lights on the board. Thirty-eight miles per hour. "See," he said, "I told you forty-five was fast."

"You beat the girls," I remarked.

"Well, of course I beat the girls!" he said.

T.J. bought me a hot dog, a soda, and some taffy and we wandered toward the lake looking for picnic tables.

JEAN Blasiar

"I'll take you for a canoe ride, Em."

There was a very long line for canoes. While we waited we finished the hot dogs and drink and about half the taffy. T.J. said he hated waiting in lines, but he was willing to wait for a canoe.

Finally it was our turn. The man at the dock said he'd watch my Kewpie doll while we were out on the lake. He held the boat while T.J. got in the front and I got in the back. The canoe wobbled, but the man held onto it while we got in. He warned us not to stand up or lean over to one side. T.J. nodded his head back and forth like, "Yeah, yeah."

We each had an oar. We weren't very far out when I noticed that the canoe kept turning left, favoring the side where T.J. was paddling. I had to row harder and faster to compensate for the constant pull to the left.

The lake was crowded with canoes, but we managed to row around most of them and head for the island around the bend. We pretended that the island was inhabited by wildlife and cannibals. I was the Indian maiden searching for coconuts (like there were palm trees in Ohio!) and T.J. was the Indian hunter searching for a wild animal to shoot with his bow and arrow. He also fished for the "big one," listing dangerously once or twice to pull in a whopper. I had to shift my weight to starboard every time he leaned left.

"Look there!" T.J. said. He was pointing at lilies float-ing just ahead of us. "I'll get you one, Em."

What T.J. didn't know but learned soon enough is that lilies don't just float. They're connected at the bottom of the pond or lake by roots, and when T.J. leaned out the front of the canoe to grab for the lily, it was just enough to capsize the canoe, flipping both of us into the water.

I, unfortunately, wound up under the boat with my pigtail caught under the seat. I must have hit my head on something, the edge of the boat or the oar or something, because everything went black for a few seconds. Then when I realized that I was trapped under the boat, I had to tug at my pigtail with all my might and push myself down to get away from the boat, which was in the water bottom up.

I guess while I was underwater T.J. panicked and was screaming my name. I found out later that he'd gone under several times searching for me. It was murky and full of lily pad roots underwater, so I guess he didn't see me when I emerged on the other side of the canoe.

The last time T.J. came up for air, he saw me clinging to the bottom of the boat.

"The sign at the dock said *NO SWIMMING*," I remarked coolly, wiping the water out of my face.

T.J. splashed a huge amount of water at me with the heel of his hand.

JEAN Blasiar

"I think this boat may be sinking," I said. "What do you think?"

But before T.J. could answer, someone on a bullhorn on a fast-approaching speedboat began shouting at us.

"Can you tread," T.J. said, "till they get here?"

"I hold the record in junior aquatics," I said boastfully. T.J. shook his head and raised his eyes. I know he didn't believe me.

After we were helped into the powerboat and were sitting inside the cabin, wrapped in blankets—wet pigtails dripping down my blanket—T.J. turned to me and said, "What was that baloney about you holding some record treading water?" He picked up one of my pigtails and squeezed the water out of it.

"I do," I admitted. "Why are we sitting under these blankets?"

"So we don't catch cold."

"But our clothes are dripping. Why don't we let the sun dry them?"

"Don't confuse these guys," T.J. whispered. "Shut up and be rescued. They don't know that you're some champion water treader."

The guys who brought us in insisted that we go to the first aid station because of a bump on my forehead. I insisted on stopping to pick up my Kewpie doll first. Fortunately at the dock, the guy who had helped us was out on the lake trying to haul in his submerged canoe when I picked up my doll.

T.J. and I hightailed it over to the first aid station. Jane and Mike came running in shortly after we arrived. They'd been watching the commotion on the lake and then realized that the two kids who had capsized out there were us.

Jane fussed over me and Mike checked out T.J.

"I'm okay," T.J. kept saying.

A nurse in the first aid station applied an ice bag to my head and told me to hold it while she rummaged through some clothes in a basket and came up with two sets of overalls and a couple of T-shirts.

Mike asked me what size shoes I wore and he went out to try to find a pair for T.J. and myself. After I had lain down for about ten minutes with the ice bag, Mike returned with two pairs of flip-flops.

Jane found a plastic bag for our wet clothes. I thanked the nurse for the ice bag, which she insisted I take with me and which I dumped into the first trash can I found outside.

"Come on, Chip and Dale," Mike said when we left the first aid station. "See if you can keep up with the old folks this time."

It was a great afternoon. We talked Jane into skipping the fancy lunch and pigging out instead on frosty whips, popcorn, and ice cream.

We watched an aerial show and then Jane wanted to sample the homemade jams. Mike went with her.

"Let's ride some horses," T.J. said. He did ride a fairly frisky young mare around the track while I watched, *again*.

"Wow," he said, climbing down. "That isn't for girls."

"What else do *you* want to do?" I asked sarcastically. He didn't even notice.

"Let's try the horseshoes," he said, walking on.

I was beginning to feel like the little Kewpie doll I carried—a hollow, redheaded, glittery-eyes piece of plaster with a painted smile on its face.

"Six horseshoes for fifty cents," the barker yelled.

T.J. didn't get a horseshoe anywhere near the peg. The barker handing out the horseshoes turned to me as we were leaving. "Try your luck, little lady," he said.

I smiled at T.J. and handed him the Kewpie doll to hold. Then I nailed that peg with the horseshoe. "Let's have a big hand for the little lady, folks," the barker shouted. He handed me a key ring in the shape of a horseshoe, which I gave to T.J. and took back my doll.

"Let's ride something," I suggested.

"Boy, what a lucky throw," T.J. said, putting the key ring in his pocket. "This is really a neat key ring, Em."

Lucky throw!

"Beat you at skeeball," I said.

"You're on."

Usually, skeeball is my specialty. The object, of course, is to roll a ball about the size of a tennis ball up a slope and into one of the rings. I got two in the fifty ring, one in the hundred ring, and one in the gutter.

"Can't do a thing with my arm when it gets wet," I alibied.

T.J. got three in the fifty ring and one in the hundred.

"So…" I conceded that one. "Darts?"

"Hey, Emmy!" someone behind us called.

T.J. and I both turned around. I was afraid that I recognized that voice and I was right. It was Dan Spears, a classmate of mine and a real jerk.

"Was that you who fell in the lake?" Dan said. "I told these guys with me that I bet that was you. Nobody has pigtails like yours."

"Dan," I said, "this is T.J. Blake. Dan Spears."

T.J. nodded to Dan.

"We were just leaving," I said, walking slowly toward the door of the arcade.

"Why didn't you swim ashore?" Dan chided me. "You need the practice."

"Ha-ha. See you around, Dan." I walked farther away. "Ready, T.J.?"

T.J. followed me out the door. He had to hurry to keep

up. I was trying to put lots of space between us and Dan Spears.

"How about some cotton candy?" I suggested.

"What'd he mean by that?" T.J. wanted to know.

"What'd he mean by what?"

"You need the practice."

"Oh. He's a jerk."

"But what did he mean by that?"

"How should I know? We're both on the swimming team. He's always mouthing off about something."

"Really?"

"Really. I told you, he's a jerk."

"Not that. You're on the swim team?"

"Yes. Are you going to buy me some cotton candy or not?"

"Sure."

We stopped at the cotton candy booth. T.J. bought two.

"Thanks," I said, filling my mouth with a big piece so I wouldn't have to talk.

"Then you really weren't afraid of drowning out there," T.J. said.

I thought, *He's disappointed that I wasn't afraid.* "Good swimmers drown, too, you know," I said with a mouthful.

"But why did you stay under so long?"

"Why did I stay under so long? Because my pigtail was

caught under the seat, dummo! What did you think? I'm on the swim team. I don't hold any records for underwater survival." Actually, I do. "Did you think I was faking so you'd have to dive down and save me or some dumb thing like that?"

"Don't get mad."

"I'm not mad." I was mad.

"It's just that I was worried about you when you didn't come up right away."

"I'm glad you were worried about me. I was worried about me, too, for a few seconds under that canoe."

We were walking along slowly, but we'd been shouting at each other and people were staring.

"I have a feeling that you're not as fragile as you look," T.J. said unexpectedly.

"Who said I was fragile?"

"But you were scared when we jumped off that train."

"You bet. Right down to my toes."

He looked at me and smiled. "You were?"

"Yes, I was. But you weren't."

"Sure I was."

"No, you weren't. Maybe later when you realized the danger, when you thought about what *could* have happened, but not when you had to act. You weren't scared at all then. I'd still be hiding in that baggage car, sitting on

JEAN Blasiar

that big bag of spikes if you hadn't dragged me off that train."

T.J. didn't say anything. We just kept walking.

"Let's ride the merry-go-round," I suggested.

T.J. looked at me like I was crazy. "What?"

"Too scary for you?"

T.J. grabbed my hand and dragged me over to the merry-go-round. We jumped on. When I reached for the strap on the horse to haul myself up, the Kewpie doll in one hand, and the cotton candy in the other, I accidentally jammed the cotton candy in my hair.

T.J. thought that was hysterical. "You redheads," he said. "You look so good in pink."

The music started. "Are you on the polo team also, jock?" T.J. shouted over the music.

"If we had one," I shouted back, "I'd be on it."

He didn't believe me. Again, he didn't believe me. But he laughed. "Wait till Jerseyville meets Franklin next year," he said.

"In what?" I said.

"Swimming."

"Oh, yeah? Don't put any money on Franklin's JV, friend."

"I wouldn't," T.J. said. "I'd put it on the varsity. I'm the captain."

I must have been sitting there with my mouth open. T.J. was laughing. "Braces don't look so good pink," he said. "Even on a redhead."

I shut my mouth instantly and ran my tongue over my braces. Swell! I forgot about cotton candy and braces. And the taffy, too.

T.J. whipped my horse with his cotton candy stick. That screwball! All summer we'd been swimming laps and he never once mentioned being on Franklin's varsity swim team. And captain!

I spied Jane and Mike walking by. Mike had his arm around Jane. I pointed them out to T.J.

"Looks like I'm going to have a new father soon," T.J. said, stealing a piece of cotton candy from my cone.

We called to Jane and Mike and asked them to join us. I was surprised when they did.

It was a neat day. Jane said that since she'd been such a good sport to go on the merry-go-round we all had to go with her to the bandstand for the concert. We traded the concert for the fancy lunch in the revolving restaurant, which neither T.J. nor I wanted to do.

We sat in the first row of the band shell and, unfortunately for Jane, right in front of the drummer. Jane lasted about twenty minutes. "Let's go!" she screamed just as the band ended abruptly and her voice and her scream were heard by everyone. Pink looks good on brunettes also.

JEAN Blasiar

Mike followed Jane out and T.J. and I lagged behind. When we were far enough away from the band that I could hear what Jane was trying to say, what she was saying was, "You stay if you want to." Of course, by then it was too late to get our seats in the first row again.

Jane and I went into the ladies' room. Jane insisted on taking my wet hair out of pigtails and brushing it. "Your hair will never dry if you leave it in those braids," she said. She tried putting it back in one pigtail, but I told her it was too heavy. Finally, she braided it again in two.

When we came out after a very long time, Mike and T.J. were riding bumper cars. Jane whispered to me, in case I had any thought about joining them, which I definitely did, that men don't go for aggressive women. Sick!

It was about five when we headed for the parking lot. It was quiet in the car on the ride home. When we were turning the corner of my street, Jane handed me the plastic bag with my wet clothes. I had my Kewpie doll. "I really want to thank you," I said to both Jane and Mike. "I…"

I looked up at our driveway and screamed. "That black car in our driveway!"

"Black car?" T.J. screamed. "Is it…is it…?"

"It's *DAD*!" I grabbed T.J. and shook him. "It's *DAD*! He's home!"

Then I leaned over the front seat and kissed both Jane and Mike.

"Thank you, Jane. Thank you, Mike," I said. I took the plastic bag, crawled over T.J., planting a kiss somewhere near his cheek, and got out of the car.

Pigtails were flying as I ran up the driveway to our house.

What a wonderful day!

What a wonderful summer!

I didn't even make headlines or anything to bring Dad home.

About the Author

Jean Blasiar is an author and playwright with eight full-length productions in the Los Angeles area, one of which was optioned by Twentieth Century Fox for a pilot. She is the author of seven Young Adult novels, including the Emmy Budd Tween Detective series.

Mrs. Blasiar resides in Southern California where she is at work on her fifth Emmy novel, *Emmy Budd and the Scarlet Scarf.*